Susan Essel

Running into the Arms of God

D0580467

To William and Monica Hannon,
my parents, who were my first teachers in the faith
and who by word and example
taught me how to pray.

Running into the Arms of God

STORIES OF PRAYER ◆ PRAYER AS STORY

To Susan and Eamon, God Bless,

PATRICK HANNON

Pat Hannon, cc

acta
PUBLICATIONS

Running into the Arms of God
Stories of Prayer/Prayer as Story
by Patrick Hannon, CSC

Editing by Gregory F. Augustine Pierce
Design and Typesetting by Larry Taylor Design, Ltd.
Cover image by Joaquin Palting

Quotations from the Psalms used on the section title pages are from the New Revised Standard Version of the Bible, copyright © 1989 by the Division of Christian Education of the National Council of the Churches of Christ in the USA. All rights reserved. Used by permission.

Copyright © 2005 Patrick Hannon, CSC

Published by ACTA Publications, 5559 W. Howard Street, Skokie, IL 60077, 800-397-2282, www.actapublications.com

Library of Congress Catalog number: 2005929649

ISBN: 0-87946-295-7 (hardcover)
         0-87946-292-2 (softcover)

Printed in the United States of America

Year: 10 09 08 07 06 05   Printing: 10 9 8 7 6 5 4 3 2 1

Contents

Foreword: Inky Sinuous Prayers 7

Prologue: Those Crazy Irish Monks 10

Matins: Three in the Morning/Waiting 17

   In the Springtime of Life 18

   The Woman Never Sleeps 21

   Staring Down the Darkness Together 26

Lauds: Five in the Morning/Praise 31

   Making Donuts 32

   Brothers 37

   The City Prays 43

Prime: Six in the Morning/Work 49

   Working in Eden 50

   Breakfast with God 55

   A Soul Kissed 60

Terce: Nine in the Morning/The Holy Spirit 65

   Intoxication 66

   Running into the Arms of God .70

Sext: Noontime/Silence 73

   Silent Soldiers 74

None: Three in the Afternoon/Eucharist 79

   A Portion of Bread, A Drop of Wine 80

   Boxing Gloves 83

   Interviewing the Dog 87

Vespers: Sunset/Family .93

   The Long Way Home 94

   California Highway 39 98

   Family Values 106

Compline: Nine in the Evening/Completion 111

   Whittling the Legs Down 112

   One Pitcher, One Batter, One Second in Kane County, Illinois 117

   The Last Word 123

Epilogue: Prayer as an Exercise in Metaphor 127

Foreword

Inky Sinuous Prayers

Let's cut to the chase. Why bother to read this book? There are a thousand reasons not to, and some of those reasons are mighty good ones.

But I tell you there are stories that matter in these pages. There are stories that are real food. There are stories you won't forget for a long time.

Here are stories that are inky sinuous prayers. Here are lines and passages and images and tales that will make you laugh and weep and wince and howl and sit up straight.

Here is an honest man, which is a pleasure to see and to hear and to contemplate. Here is a teacher, which is a brave thing to be these days. Here is someone who has swum in dark seas and emerged alone to tell thee that other people saved him, which is a crucial bit of wisdom that salts and spices and sweetens all his work. Here is a writer with a weird, quirky, peculiar sense of humor, which in the end is an extraordinary form of prayer, as you know very well.

Here is an ardent baseball fan (of, hilariously, the Oakland A's, I mean, really, talk about your Sisyphean tasks) who has the strength of character to not go all gooey and blathery about baseball as metaphor for life, bless his heart.

Here is a human being who struggles to discover the divine in the laughing and weeping and muttering and banging his head against the stone moments of life, as well as in the singing and sighing and moaning and humming.

Here is a priest who understands deep in the tattered fabric of his soul that his job is to serve and not to sermonize.

Here is a teller of stories, which is an ancient vocation and responsibility and a gift of immense power and prayer. For we are all stories. We are made of stories; we swap stories all day long; we fall in love by story (some of them true); our religions are based on stories; our cultures are founded on stories; our educations are skeins of story; our memories are constructed of stories; our souls are story-verbs. So to hold in your hand Pat's wriggling box of fascinating stories is to have before you mirror-bits and prism-pieces of yourself, your life, your experiences. And it's Pat's gift that his very personal stories are not so much finally about Pat Hannon as they are about the extraordinary possibility and stuttering poetry of Us—brave and cruel, generous and greedy, sweet and snarling, impatient and open, exhilarated and exhausted, holier than we can ever fully see.

Once in a while our eyes open for a flash of a shard of an instant, stunned open by a song or a face or a death or a birth or a crash or a creature or a story, and we see things as they really are, stitched together in a vast coherence by what for total lack of better word we call God. It is my conviction, having read and heard and pondered Pat Hannon's stories for fifteen years, that one or more of them will startle you into epiphany.

Sometimes on this particular planet there are stories that break your heart and make you laugh or think and shove you gently but insistently toward your best self. Flannery O'Connor and Isaac Bashevis Singer and Andre Dubus and J.F. Powers and Primo Levi and Frank O'Connor wrote that kind of story; and Annie Dillard and Barry Lopez and Cynthia Ozick and David Duncan do now. So does Patrick Hannon, a young Holy Cross priest shuffling toward the Christ he sees in everyone.

Trust me. Go ahead. Open the book. Don't even finish listening to me. Crack this sucker open and start with the "The City Prays," maybe, or maybe the bread and wine essay, and then I bet you will just keep wandering down the papery road with Pat, swapping stories. That will be a graceful prayer, yes it will, and it will jolt the universe forward two inches toward the Light, which is the point.

Brian Doyle
University of Portland
Portland, Oregon

Prologue

Those Crazy Irish Monks

We were on top of a rock seven miles off the Dingle Peninsula of Ireland. It was not unlike a Chicago morning in February, except this was late June. A cold, wet mist of gray seemed to seep into every nook and cranny of the Skellig named for Saint Michael. We had taken a forty-five minute boat ride out to a rock that climbed nearly eight hundred feet into the Atlantic brume. Having left very early that morning to get to the boat on time, we were quite hungry: seven teenaged boys, a fellow Holy Cross priest, another teacher from our school, and me. Halfway up the rock I could tell the boys were famished, because when I told them not to worry, that there was a McDonald's at the top, they actually believed me. So by the time we got to the top and had a chance to inspect the remains of the ancient monastery constructed there, they were more than just a little disgusted with me. I had promised them food, and unless I was willing to turn stones—from which there was a multitude to choose—into Big Macs and Quarter Pounders with Cheese, they were just going to ignore me.

For my part, I was more than just a little disappointed in them. Here we were, in the Atlantic Ocean, on top of a huge rock towering eight hundred feet in the air, investigating the nearly unmolested remains of a monastery over 1400 years old, built by Irish monks with quarried rock and nothing else, and all they could think about was their empty bellies. Not exactly a Kodak moment.

I did my best to get them interested in the monastery and its history—the genius of ancient Celtic engineering and design that kept the dozen or so beehive-shaped structures sturdy and dry; the faith and the courage of the men who built them and made this place their home—but they would hear none of it. I retreated into one of the larger structures, which was once used by the community of monks as its chapel, and stood there alone for a few minutes. I touched the cold stone of the curved wall, closed my eyes, and imagined the chapel filled with a dozen sleepy monks with growling bellies chanting the psalms of Matins in Latin. I opened my eyes and looked out through the small opening in front of me. Standing by itself with the blue sea as a backdrop was a Celtic cross, and it struck me that it was because of that cross—or more accurately the man Jesus who had once hung upon one—that a collection of crazy Irish monks got it in their minds to row out here and harvest heavy rock with nothing but simple tools and simple faith and build a home in the sky where, having inched their way just a little closer to God, they could pray in peace. Touching the walls of the chapel, I prayed for a fraction of their faith—and their patience—as I went to round up the guys for the trek back to the boat.

A few days later while we were at dinner at a nice restaurant in Dublin, I noticed that one of the guys, John by name, had been absent for a while. I assumed he had gone off to sneak a pint, or a cigarette, or both, but I figured ten minutes was more than enough time for him to be gone. I found him leaning against the wall outside, taking drags from a cigarette, looking out at the sun slowly setting over sylvan hills in the distance. He cut a rather pensive pose against that dusky sky, so I approached him slowly, choosing to wait for him to speak first.

"You know, Father, I've been sort of lost lately," he began, his eyes focused and touched with a shadow of sadness, as if he were seeing the truth of his life for the very first time. "I know I have done things that I haven't been very proud of, that I've made mistakes." He took a drag from his cigarette. And then he looked at me.

"When we were up at the top of that rock a few days ago," John continued, "I was in the room that was the monks' chapel. I don't know what it was, but something just came over me. I realized I had gotten really far away from God, that I had chosen to walk away from him. I don't even remember the last time I've been to Sunday Mass." John took another puff from his cigarette. And then he said something I will never forget: "Father, right there, in that chapel, I just started to cry. The distance just seemed too great. And so I prayed to God and said: 'Find me.' Father, I don't know what happened, but I felt something deep inside, like God actually heard me." And with one last puff on the cigarette, flicking it into the street as if it were some shell of a former life he was leaving behind, John said, "Now I know things are going to be different." He paused and looked up and added cautiously, "At least I hope so," in tacit recognition that it wouldn't be easy.

John had the heart of a crazy Irish monk. I like to think that we all have such hearts. For we hunger still for the same things that those Irish monks hungered for so long ago—a hunger that growled and stirred, a deep hunger that found them perched on top of a rock in the middle of an ocean—just to be an inch closer to God. For us, it is a hunger maybe for peace and contentment, maybe for forgiveness and mercy, maybe for love and companionship. The hunger of the human heart has a thousand faces. But it is, in the end, always a hunger for God. It is a hunger that creeps up on us after we have been on the road for a long time, and it will not be sated by fast food for the soul. Like John, most of us find it quite easy to get lost along the way, and then, when our compass is shattered and we find that we recognize nothing or no one around us, not even ourselves, that hunger becomes prayer, for it articulates the longing for home better than words could ever do. All prayer says, in so many words, what John once whispered secretly in a stone chapel eight hundred feet in the air seven miles off the coast of Ireland: "Find me."

The Irish wordsmith Patrick Kavanagh in his poem "The Great Hunger" wrote: "God is in the bits and pieces of Everyday—A kiss here and a laugh again, and sometimes tears, A pearl necklace round the neck of poverty." It *is* in kisses and laughter and sometimes tears that we come face to face with the God who loves us, and it seems that only when we are hungriest are we willing to feast upon divinity.

That is what this collection of stories is all about, stories that can readily be distilled down to a simple prayer of heartfelt hunger: Find me.

The lasting image we have of Jesus in the Gospel of Luke is of a man hanging on a cross, clinging to a Father's promise that he would not be forgotten, that his death would not be the last word. Luke invites us to pay close attention to the whispered prayer of the one next to Jesus, who clearly had found himself lost and far from his true home, a man who had done things he probably was not very proud of. That man, the Good Thief, whom the tradition names *Dismas* (which means "dying"), asked Jesus if he might find it in his heart to come back and find him and bring him home too. And Jesus whispered, "This day you will be with me in paradise."

"Find me!" a teenaged boy whispered in secret in a dark chapel on a lonely rock miles from nowhere. It might be our prayer, too, as we take stock from time to time of where we have been and where we wish to go. For it is prayer that reminds us that there is no place too far, too high, too dark, or too secret for God to find us and bring us home.

Those crazy Irish monks. They gathered in a chapel of stone faithfully eight times a day to pray, moments that punctuated the hours in such a way that left no one mistaken: every moment holds forth the possibility of our being found by the God of Creation who because of His very nature searches us out. We who occupy a different time and a different space from theirs are no different.

The chapters in this book are divided into the eight prayers that those crazy Irish monks prayed every single day while they lived and worked on the top of that rock. They serve to remind us that every moment is holy and that, believe it or not, we probably pray more than we realize. They serve as guiding lights for the stories I tell, each one touched with the particular color and tone of the prayer it seeks to amplify; they guide us through one day, which for God, as the psalmist tells us, is like a thousand days. We may not be crazy enough to live on top of a rock and pray through the day and night. God knows I'm not. But we are tethered to the same earth by the same soulful hunger that found its voice in a teenaged boy who dared to ask, to beg, "Find me." Once we ask, God will. The Good Thief taught us that.

Patrick Hannon, CSC
Chicago, Illinois
Good Friday, 2005

CHAPTER ONE

Matins
Three in the Morning
Waiting

Hear, O LORD, when I cry aloud, be gracious to me and answer me!

"Come," my heart says, "seek his face!" Your face, LORD, do I seek.

Do not hide your face from me. Do not turn your servant away in anger, you who have been my help.

Do not cast me off; do not forsake me, O God of my salvation!

I believe that I shall see the goodness of the LORD in the land of the living.

Wait for the LORD; be strong, and let your heart take courage; wait for the LORD!

Psalm 27

I In the Springtime of Life

"I don't think I'm going to make it through this." We hear those words spoken a thousand times in a lifetime. Heck, my friend Steve Kotz uttered them every day in Dr. Bonhorst's painfully tedious environmental science class our sophomore year of college. But nothing prepares you for the first time you really hear those words from someone you love and know you're going to lose.

It was around three in the morning, and I was sitting next to Tessa's bed in her hospital room, dimly lit with that unnatural hospital fluorescent gleam. Van Morrison music from the CD player in the corner gently lulled me into a kind of unstudied peace, a temporary parole from pain that comes sometimes in the middle of the night. The vigil had begun a few days before, when reality finally snapped the last thread of hope, and Tessa's mom and dad, her three sisters, my sister Julie (Tessa's closest friend), and I set up sentry duty so Tessa would never be alone. No one had yet had a heart-to-heart talk with Tessa about her impending death. Not her parents or sisters. Not her doctor or my sister. Not me.

I had been touched by death before, but this one was particularly tough. One minute Tessa is at the top of her game: an accountant for a big accounting firm in Portland, Oregon, young, talented, at peace with her life. The next minute she is diagnosed with a particularly nasty cancer that would take her in seven months. Her steady march toward death had the effect of stopping me in my tracks. She was five years younger than I, but both of us had lived a sufficient amount of time to appreciate the tenuous grip with which we humans grasp the reins of life. But now she was going to be on one side of life and I was going to be on the other. At three

> NOTHING PREPARES YOU FOR THE FIRST TIME YOU REALLY HEAR THOSE WORDS FROM SOMEONE YOU LOVE AND KNOW YOU'RE GOING TO LOSE.

o'clock one early morning, Tessa whispered to me, "I don't think I'm going to make it through this." And with those words she reached back across that line, hoping to grasp my hand.

That reaching across, that grasping, was a prayer. So was the encompassing darkness, the Van Morrison music, the fluorescent light over the bed, the hushed admission all wrapped up together. I reached over and held Tessa's hand, but I couldn't think of one thing to say. I just looked at her and nodded and smiled a smile I hoped would convey what words could not. And my feeble smile, too, was prayer.

Sometimes the best prayers are those unspoken. By "best" I don't mean the prayers God answers first. No, the best prayers are the ones that get us to believe again in those truths we had judged to be false or ridiculous or impossible. The best prayers reconnect us to God and thus to each other and our true selves. The best prayers are like quiet earthquakes that sneak up on us and change everything. At three o'clock

19

in the morning, both Tessa and I were praying without uttering a syllable. Our bodies were doing the talking, and God had no need of words or sound to do the listening.

Tessa had already crossed the line. She and I were experiencing life from different sides, but even then—in the middle of the night—the line that seemingly separates life from death, despair from hope, suffering from joy, was disappearing. Reaching across the divide, we both held fast to the eternal promise of God that once stiffened the resolve of the Crucified One and has fortified the quivering human heart through all of history ever since. We are never alone, Jesus taught us, even in the midst of our own death.

IT IS A COURAGEOUS PRAYER BECAUSE IT IS OUR WAY OF STARING DOWN THE DARKNESS.

"Into your hands I commend my spirit," he prayed confidently, and we can as well.

It is a courageous prayer because it is our way of staring down the darkness. It is a prayer that draws its breath from silent hope and constant faith and clings fast to the promise made by the Living God to his beloved son. In life, as in death, we are never alone.

The Woman Never Sleeps II

Most children grow up believing that mothers have eyes in the back of their heads and ears that can eavesdrop through walls of thick cinderblock. That's a given. My mother once came into the room literally seconds after my brothers and I had quietly settled on a wicked plan to terrorize the neighborhood with water balloons later that afternoon, looked at us calmly, studied our faces, took a drag from her cigarette, and then matter-of-factly stated, "None of you are leaving the house today."

My mother also almost never slept. This unsettling, sobering truth was passed down from older brother to younger brother in a tone that said in so many words: If you want to live, you'd better believe it. Still, we were like cats, my brothers and I—nothing really good got started until the lights were turned off, the doors were locked, and Mom and Dad were asleep.

Dad was never an issue. It seemed that he was in bed by eight every night. Sometimes he purposely locked Mom out of the bedroom, feigning connubial petulance because his wife was not coming to bed with him. We all would sit around the living room, enjoying the unfolding drama: Dad "demanding" that wife come to bed; wife refusing; door being slammed shut and locked; wife demanding to be let in a couple of hours later; husband snoring loudly on the other side; wife having to fetch the key.

Eventually, Mom would go to bed. We brothers listened, snooped, ran reconnaissance missions, reported back, double-checked, and then and only then entertained the possibility of sneaking out of the house. But she was a formidable obstacle, our mother. Some of the time she stopped us in our tracks before we even had the chance to fly the coop. Mostly though, she caught us on the way back into the house. She'd paddle our little behinds before they had the chance to make it completely through the bedroom window. Thankfully, children have shallow memories. So soon after Mom released us on our own recognizance, we were back at the drawing board, planning and conniving, determined to evade her finely calibrated global positioning system.

One evening my brothers Mike and Greg decided to take our mom's station wagon out for a spin. The idea was hatched (like most of our

> MOSTLY I REMEMBER NOT GETTING CAUGHT, WHICH WAS UNUSUAL IN ITSELF.

schemes) in the spirit of healthy brotherly competition. Greg was convinced that he was the better driver. Mike was adamant that he, a year older, had much more talent in the matter. I stayed out of the fray, content to let my older brothers, twelve and thirteen respectively, duke it out on their own. It was decided that later that night we would push Mom's car down the street a bit, so not to stir our mother from her slumber. I was to go along as impartial judge.

I honestly cannot recall who the better driver was, though I do remember Greg driving on the median of the boulevard by mistake and Mike cussing him out. I remember our driving through the pickup windows at McDonald's, Jack in the Box and Burger King and making a passing sweep through the parking lot at our grade school. But mostly I remember not getting caught, which was unusual in itself. We returned the car to the place Mom had parked it and readjusted the driver's seat and rear view mirror to the best of our ability. We wiped the car clean of fingerprints and snuck through our bedroom window with adrenaline sufficient for an army of ancient Celtic warriors.

It was our greatest triumph to date. Somehow we knew the next morning that we had feasted at the table of the gods and that all subsequent sojourns would be pathetic exercises by comparison. Mom took drags from her cigarette and long sips from her cup of coffee that morning. She dished out mush to her brood and brushed the girls' hair. She barked out orders in her usual cadence and tone of exasperation. And she was none the wiser.

Well, not exactly. Years later my brothers and sisters and I were sitting around the kitchen table with Mom, reminiscing about our childhood exploits. Figuring some statute of limitations had expired, we told Mom of that early morning joy ride down the boulevard, but it turned out to be she who surprised us. Mom knew we had snuck out that night, that we had taken the car, that we had returned it, and that we had clumsily restored its interior to some semblance of its previous order. How did she know? Don't ask me. She never let on. And why we had not been sentenced to some Australian penal colony, being the Irish miscreants that we were, remains an even greater mystery to all of us to this day.

As it was, Mom had chosen to remain silent and awake that night. She may have been in bed. She may have closed her eyes. She may have been tempted by sleep's alluring, slumberous song. But our mother—like most, if not all, mothers—stayed awake until she knew, in the same way God knows, that her children were home and safe. And this silent waiting is a prayer more powerful than any string of words.

Saint Teresa of Avila once wrote, "Prayer is nothing else than a conversation between two persons who love one another." On those nights when children are out and their parents are awake until they come home, I suspect that a mother's or a father's heart speaks to God as a fellow parent.

> I SUSPECT THAT A MOTHER'S OR A FATHER'S HEART SPEAKS TO GOD AS A FELLOW PARENT.

I am reminded of this every time I read the parable of the Prodigal Son. Though the context of the story is one of human sin and divine mercy, I am always left with the image of the loving father waiting with an aching and longing heart for his child to return home. On the surface, the fierce protective predilection mothers and fathers harbor for their children may seem mere creaturely instinct, something we share with the rest of the animal kingdom. But I think its source is reflective of the divine spark that animates our souls and draws us always back to the God whose love for us—like a mother's or a father's love—is unwavering and unconditional.

When we all grew old enough to stay out late, Mom would put a check-in sheet on the table by the front door. The last one in had to lock the door, turn off the lights, make sure the cat was out, and—most importantly—make sure the Mr. Coffee in the kitchen was set to percolate at six in the morning. We all assumed this system was to give Mom permission to actually go to sleep, but whenever I was the last to return home, I'd perform the chores, head for bed, get to Mom and Dad's room, and quietly open the door to see if Mom was actually asleep. Every single time, I'd hear her say, "Goodnight, Pat, go to bed now." The woman who never slept must have been able to judge by the sound of our footsteps who was returning home when.

Whether they realize it or not, in their patient waiting for their children to return home, in their staying awake long into the night, parents become yet another incarnation of God's love, not only for their children but also for the world. Saint Elizabeth of the Trinity had a favorite prayer that mirrors the kind of prayer mothers and fathers pray—even if they don't know they're praying it: "Consuming fire! Spirit of love! Descend within me and reproduce within me as it were an incarnation of the Word, that I may be to God another humanity wherein He renews His mystery."

My mother stayed awake every night until the last of her children was home safe and sound. She prayed in secret, and God, Parent to us all, listened and understood. Prayer is, after all, a conversation between two persons who love each other.

III

Staring Down the Darkness Together

At first my brothers and sisters and I thought Mary was just getting fat.

On any given day in the Hannon house, you could find seven or eight spoons dug into a tub of Rocky Road or mint chip ice cream tucked away in the freezer in the garage behind the hamburger and pork chops. These spoons, left behind by my brothers and sisters and me, stood as mocking evidence to our mother that nothing, not even threat of punishment, could stand between the sacred ice cream and her sugar-starved children. Once, in desperation, Mom actually put a lock on the freezer. She kept the key on a chain around her neck. An emergency meeting of the kids was called, and it was decided that Greg would unfasten the screws and then ditch the lock in the garbage can at the side of the house. He had the Craftsman toolbox, the know-how, and the reputation for getting into the most trouble anyway. That evening, four quarts of vanilla and chocolate ice cream were liberated. Mom waved the white flag. But it did take Dad and his sweet tooth a whole month to prevail upon her to start buying ice cream again, which she finally did. The spoons arrived soon after.

One of these spoons had to belong to Mary. How else could you explain the gain in weight, tightening waistline, and tacky clothes? Even in the fashion-challenged days of the mid-1970s, Mary was the chic model in the family, enjoying a slim figure, feathered hair, and soft, milky skin that had never known Clearasil. But in that summer of 1978, she dressed like a chimney sweep. When she wasn't cooped up in her room listening to her Fleetwood Mac albums, she was holed up in the bathroom for hours at a time. I can remember two or three times when we almost secured the services of Greg and his toolbox again to dismantle the doorknob of that bathroom.

THIS WAS AN ADVENT MOMENT IN SUMMER SEASON.

We would pound on the door, screaming for mercy, begging her to let us in; finally, Mary would storm out of the bathroom, her mascara running down her cheeks, cussing at us and telling us all to drop dead. Back to her bedroom, door slammed, Fleetwood Mac blaring through the keyhole—we merely thought she was hitting the ice cream stash a little too hard.

One afternoon, however, my mother and older sister Sally knocked on her door. They were in there for an hour or longer. By this time word had gotten around in the house that it wasn't ice cream that accounted for Mary's weight gain. Our sister Mary, all of eighteen years old and unmarried, was going to have a baby. She had spent the better part of six months carrying a child in her womb and the weight of worry in her heart all by herself. The three of them emerged from the room wiping tears from their eyes. Sally had taken a brush and brought some shine and sheen back into

Mary's hair. Mom held Mary's shoulders and told her everything was going to be all right. Dad had been summoned from work and had arrived home. Only once in my whole life have I ever seen my father cry, and it was when he came through the front door that day and saw his daughter being held by his wife.

It seemed that Mary was willing to give the baby up for adoption, but that didn't seem to sit too well with my father's soul and his Hannon pride.

"Mary," we whose ears were pressed against her bedroom door could hear him say, "if you want to give the baby up for adoption, that's fine; then your mother and I will adopt the baby." The words came out softly, reaching over a canyon of fear and hurt and worry and disappointment, like a bridge of tears uniting them. Fathers and daughters share a special bond, it seems, and we all witnessed the strength of that bond that afternoon.

If Advent is the season in which good Christians tilt their heads to the rising sun in joyful hope at the dawn of new life, well, this was an Advent moment in summer season. Mary was pregnant, Dad was crying, Mom was blowing her nose into her apron, Sally was already on the phone calling aunts and uncles, Julie (the youngest) was trying to feel the baby kick in her sister's belly. Her brothers, acting under the suspicion that this was not a second Immaculate Conception, were trying to figure out what we would say (and do) to Mary's boyfriend when he came by later that day. All the while, Grandma sat in her rocking chair, knitting away, seemingly oblivious to everything that was going on. It was like the whole world had turned upside down and inside out. When we all had a chance to catch our breath, the conversation turned to the two most important questions at hand: What were we going to name the baby, and should we buy more ice cream right away?

Early the next morning—really in the middle of the night—my sister made her way to the kitchen for a cup of coffee (Mary told me this years later). At the kitchen table, she and my grandmother, who by then had basically become a nocturnal creature, sat. It was around half past three, lights were dimmed in the house, and the kitchen was cast in shadow save for the small light over the stove. In my mind's eye, I see two women—one old and wise, one young and frightened—speaking in hushed tones, sipping coffee. Grandma must have been handing over to Mary wisdom purchased over a lifetime of triumphs and tragedies.

> THIS IS WHERE THE GOSPEL AND THE PRAYER IT INSPIRES TAKES ON FLESH.

They sat there for what seemed a very long time, with Grandma holding Mary's hand and gazing into her granddaughter's eyes, never seeming to waver or pause. She must have spoken of hope and promise with the confidence of a woman who had seen a lot of grace and gravity in her life. She must have told Mary of the joy only a woman with a life stirring in her belly can feel.

Looking back on that early morning, it strikes me now that this is where the gospel and the prayer it inspires takes on flesh. In a very real sense, Grandma was my sister's Gabriel—a midwife of hope, an angel sent by God in the middle of the night to ask my sister to trust Him, to hand over her fears and regrets to Him, and to believe that He would keep all His promises. My sister Mary learned to trust that night in a deeper way, much as her namesake must have learned to trust so long ago when she sat with her own angel.

It is good to know that Jesus was conceived in such trust, that he slept in such a womb of faith. It is a source of deep satisfaction to me to know that this is the way God chose to enter the world: a babe stirring in the belly of a young woman who trusted God with every fiber of her being, believing that there is no darkness so deep that it could ever suffocate the light of hope and promise.

As people of prayer tethered still to this tilting earth, we are an Advent human tribe, people accustomed to feeling hopeful anticipation, even if that hope is laced with a sometimes painful longing mixed with worry.

This is the story of our Christian faith. It begins with a young woman, bulging at the belly, sitting with an angel through the night. And it ends with a young man emerging from the darkness of a tomb and into the dawn of a new day. From beginning to end, the message rings true: God can be trusted; God keeps his promises; and those of us who find ourselves lost, alone and enveloped by the dark need only someone to sit with us and remind us that there is no darkness so deep that an angel cannot scatter it.

CHAPTER TWO

Lauds
Five in the Morning
Giving Praise

My heart is steadfast, O God, my heart is steadfast. I will sing and make melody.

Awake, my soul! Awake, O harp and lyre! I will awake the dawn.

I will give thanks to you, O LORD, among the peoples;

I will sing praises to you among the nations.

For your steadfast love is as high as the heavens; your faithfulness extends to the clouds.

Be exalted, O God, above the heavens. Let your glory be over all the earth.

Psalm 57

I Making Donuts

I suddenly remember a Dunkin' Donuts commercial from years ago. A frumpy, middle-aged man dressed in boxers and a tank top rallies each early morning with the words: "Time to make the donuts." He spoke to my generation. But then again, that early-rising, blue-collar working stiff spoke for just about all of us who find ourselves at dawn's breaking—plugging in the coffee maker, assembling the kids' sack lunches, sitting in the frigid car waiting for the engine to warm up, or making our way down darkened streets to the subway or bus stop. It's not exactly a pretty picture, but for most of us it's reality. The Norman Rockwells of the world may, with broad sentimental strokes, paint a rosier picture of six A.M., but most of us would rather just stay in bed for another hour.

> IF YOU EVER WANT TO KNOW THE DIMENSIONS OF HELL, VISIT THE UNDERPASS.

Yet the tradition of the Church has always been that early morning is the time to give praise to God, to take the stringed instruments of our hearts and serenade the God of creation with songs of joy. (Well, no one ever said prayer was going to be easy.)

Of course, there are amazingly joyful moments in life born of deeply satisfying experiences: birthdays, anniversaries, weddings, a hole in one, an afternoon at the beach, the 1989 Oakland A's World Championship. At times like these—when for a brief, precious moment we

are reminded that life really is good and that most people really are good and that God really
is good—we understand perfectly what Saint Augustine meant when he said, "We are an
Easter people and Alleluia is our song."

The Christian understanding of joy, however, goes much deeper. C.S. Lewis thought such joy
often comes to us unexpectedly and always as a gift. Someone once made a distinction between
happiness and joy that I found very instructive and wise. Happiness is a wonderful feeling, but
it is transitory and somewhat dependent upon human action for its life, sustenance and
endurance. Joy, on the other hand, cannot be manufactured by human hands. It is not so much
a feeling as it is a state of being to which we are invited without charge by God. In a way, it is
an invitation to experience the divine in the here and now—God in the moment. This kind of
joy comes when we least expect it. It is God's way of breaking through and into our lives, lest
we forget who we truly are. So it is that every new dawn—bloodshot eyes and creaky bones
notwithstanding—holds forth at least the possibility of joy worthy of morning praise.

It's around five in the morning on a Saturday. I'm on my way to pick up my newspapers at "The Shack," the clapboard, square structure where forty boys gathered
every day to roll their papers and suck down Cokes and cuss and spit and do all the
things we can never do in front of our mothers. I'm on my unreliable Huffy one-
speed, careening down dark and—by my reckoning—dangerous streets. I'm ten
years old, and I see things nobody else sees. I see creatures crouching in bushes. I
see muggers and thugs. I see my life flashing before my eyes. I cut through Strobridge
School's playground and make it down Tyee Street. I cheat death once again. As I
near The Underpass, my heart begins to beat so fast I think it's going to burst. The

Underpass. If you ever want to know the dimensions of hell, visit The Underpass. It's around forty yards long, six feet wide, and eight feet high. It is a dank, damp concrete passageway underneath Interstate 580 that connects Strobridge Avenue to Norbridge Avenue, essentially connecting the northern half of my hometown with the southern half for those willing to take a seedy shortcut.

I race down the decline and spin around the corner, knowing I have maybe five seconds to make it to the other side of hell. I'm always petrified that I'm going to run into some nefarious goon who has staked out The Underpass, waiting for a chance to strike. Well, I didn't exactly run *into* anyone. I did run *over* someone, however. He must have been some old coot sleeping it off, but I ran right over him. I screamed so loud that I am sure I woke up the dead, as well as the unfortunate soul who now had traces of bicycle tire tread on his stomach. "What the hell," I heard him utter as I screamed past him.

I cannot begin to describe the unmitigated joy I felt as I emerged from the concrete tomb that early morning. As I made my way to The Shack, I kept saying over and over again, "Thank you, God. Thank you, God," and I really meant it. I don't think I had ever felt more alive. Only the slightest hint of dawn was on the horizon, but I absorbed everything around me as if for the first time, with my eyes, ears, nose, tongue: the bark of the dueling dogs in the far distance; the backfire of a pickup truck two streets over; the feel of the grooves on the sidewalk as I raced toward Castro Valley Boulevard; the taste of morning mist that hung thick in the air; the neon lights that flickered on storefront signs.

Morning praise. Thank you, God, for giving me another day above ground. Thank you, God, for helping me not to give up the ghost. You are a good God, a merciful God, and you've got my word that I will do better.

Just up ahead, before the turn off to The Shack, is Winchell's Donuts. Much of my early life has been spent there. On weeknights, my fellow paperboys and I descend on the day-old donuts like buzzards. On mornings like this one we gather there just as Rudy the donut man is unlocking the doors so we can get the glazed donuts still warm from the deep fryer. They literally melt in your mouth. On Sundays, my three older brothers and I do our paper routes together, with Dad behind the wheel of the Ford station wagon. After the last paper is delivered we sit in one of the booths—my dad, three brothers and I, surrounded by old men and their cups of joe—and digest maple bars and cups of hot chocolate and the box scores from the sports page.

RISING FROM THE BED IS NOT UNLIKE RISING FROM THE DEAD.

I make my way down Castro Valley Boulevard and stop just alongside the plate glass window of Winchell's that lets you peer into the back where Rudy is making batches of donuts. Enveloped by a warm blanket of fluorescent light, I catch my breath. I watch Rudy as he goes about his work. You can tell by the sweat on his brow and the intensity in his eyes and the disheveled state of the apron draped around his stocky frame that he's been up since the wee hours of the morning. For just a moment it's as if he and I are the only ones awake in the whole world: I, a ten year old kid who came *this close* to wetting his pants, and Rudy, a man unafraid of anything or anyone, who gets up every morning before dawn because he knows he has a vocation to create donuts that are more than donuts, to create a space where old men and boys and the women who love them can assemble for no good reason at all except that it's morning and nothing tastes better than a chocolate old-fashion donut washed down with a cup of coffee with one cream and two sugars.

It's five in the morning, and I am praising God from the depths of my little ten-year-old heart. And I am not alone. Rudy is there as he always is, rolling the dough, punching out the holes, spreading on the glaze and the frosting. Steady. Consistent. Faithful. So it is with God. When we wake after a night of sleep, maybe our first thoughts are less than noble, tangled as they sometimes get in a web of resentment or anxiety or worry at what the day might bring. But at some point, we have to know that rising from the bed is not unlike rising from the dead. Each day holds forth both promise and peril, and it is up to each of us to decide how we will face what the day brings us. Even on those days when it seems as if we have only five seconds to make it to the other side of hell, it is still a day worthy of praise.

Brothers

Alfonso Fragassi scared the hell out of me as a kid. If I ran into him today, he'd probably still scare the hell out of me. He went by the name Alfie, but none of us ever let that kinder, gentler appellation fool us. Anyone who had a tattoo inked into his arm at the age of ten was a force to be reckoned with.

Alfie was no Eddie Haskel. Say what you will about him, but he never hid behind a façade of civility when mingling with adults. He just zipped his lip and went about the business of terrorizing the neighborhood. Every prank not attributed to one of my brothers was assumed to have been hatched by Alfie. The consensus of Arcadian Drive was that Alfie Fragassi would end up in a cell at San Quentin.

For my part, I just steered clear of him. I feared Alfie much the way the Israelites feared Yahweh, with the kind of reverential awe that clearly delineated our separate states of existence—I being assigned to mere mortal coil and Alfie seemingly transcendent, someone who could, if he so desired, crush me like a bug. Alfie had arms of oak, a chiseled jaw, and a steady gaze that betrayed not even a hint of emotion one way or the other. The most you could get out of Alfie might be a raised eyebrow every now and then or a smirk that, depending on the situation, told you he was either irritated or bemused.

Alfie attended the public school in my hometown. If memory serves me, his family was Christian of the Protestant variety. Mr. Fragassi tended to his finely manicured front lawn with a brand of medieval fanaticism that evidently fed his soul, because I never remember seeing him or his wife or Alfie ever climb into the car in their Sunday best and make it to church. I mostly saw Mrs. Fragassi through their living room window, dusting and turning couch pillows and vacuuming. Walking past the Fragassi house on a Saturday afternoon—Alfie whittling a stick with his army knife on the front stoop; his dad combing the lawn; his mother wiping her brow, a can of Pledge sticking out of her apron pocket—I found them a fascinating study, from a human anthropological perspective. Alfie's tribe was so culturally foreign to my tribe, which resided just down the street from his, that it was a minor miracle we were able to coexist at all.

You have to understand that my maternal grandmother was an O'Flaherty. I am told there is inscribed in Gaelic above the west gates of the city of Galway words that roughly translate: "Oh LORD, Deliver Us from the Fury of the O'Flahertys." It is this fierce tribal blood that flows through my veins, indeed through the veins of all my brothers and sisters. It helps explain the cuts, the bruises, the occasional shiner, and the boxing matches in the garage on Friday nights in the wintertime. By the time we moved out of the neighborhood when I was eleven, most every door in our house had to be replaced. They all had dents and holes in them, evidence of our O'Flaherty fury. I guess this was to be expected when you took the children of an Irish tribe genetically predisposed to raiding and pillaging villages and put them in a suburban, two-story house in the early 1960s. Our mother could have—without fear of embarrassment or scandal—put us all on a healthy daily regimen of Ritalin. The neighbors probably would have thrown her a party. Instead, she just drank a lot of coffee, smoked a lot of cigarettes, and held on for dear life.

In the end, what brought us together—Alfie and me—was a lake. Down the street from us at the bottom of our hill was Lake Chabot (pronounced *shu-bow*), a large, expansive reservoir

> THE REST OF US IS HIDDEN AND SECRET AND NOT EASILY EXPOSED OR EVEN SHARED.

built largely by Chinese workers in 1879, who carried buckets of dirt to build the earthen dam and then ran herds of wild mustangs back and forth to pack it down— or so the story goes. My older brothers dutifully marched down to the lake most every Saturday in the summertime before dawn. They were serious fishermen and tolerated my presence only if I brought something to occupy myself with, kept my mouth shut, and stayed out of their hair. So there I was, a pint-sized six year old with a mop of reddish-brown hair and a face full of freckles and tiny hands carrying a couple of books to read by flashlight by the lakeshore at five in the morning while my brothers, cussing in whispers, baiting hooks, munching on bologna sandwiches, and exchanging bawdy jokes, drank the sweet nectar of life. I was a boy to be pitied.

We arrived at our spot before the eastern hills even hinted of sunrise, passing the usual suspects: crusty, ancient anglers with nimble fingers still; bony men in khaki and camouflage occasionally accompanied by wives or girlfriends; and young boys with outlandish, unattainable dreams. Never underestimate the desires of a young boy with a fishing pole. My brother Greg once spent a whole morning at Lake Chabot in vain pursuit of the Big One, only to purloin three beautiful trout from an unsuspecting fisherman. Carrying them home triumphantly, Greg paraded them before his impressed—if not just a little suspicious—family.

Brian led the way that morning, tipping his head in tacit greeting as we walked by one sleepy, possessed phantom after another on our way to my brothers' favorite spot. I took my place behind them as my brothers busied themselves with setting everything up. Before too long, hooks were baited and lines were flung into the water. I sat there and watched as my brothers engaged in the time-honored male-bonding ritual that—given its universal scope—must have its origins in our cave-dwelling, prehistoric ancestors. Why else would I—not having cultivated even a passing, theoretical interest in fishing—have gotten out of bed on a summer Saturday morning?

> NEVER UNDERESTIMATE THE DESIRES OF A YOUNG BOY WITH A FISHING POLE.

The dimmest of voices, one that surely traveled the long arc of time and space, told me that this is what brothers do when they're not fighting each other. They sit by a lake in the dark and fish and let long stretches of time pass before they say anything. When they do speak, they talk about things that really matter: girls and fishing and baseball. And in time, unbeknownst to anyone, the string of whispered words, the ribald reverie, all those predawn conversations will, if you let them, entwine young souls and make a knot so tight that not even death can loosen it. Fishing with my brothers meant I was in; I was one of them. And nothing, not even my bookish leanings, could ever change that.

After a while, however, I decided to explore a little. I hadn't a watch, but it must have been close to half past five or so, because it was much lighter outside, light enough for me to venture out on my own. I knew almost every inch of that lake, the cubbyholes and caves and winding paths that often deposited you by abandoned campfires and matted patches of weeds, evidence of traveling tramps or horny teenagers. Imagine my surprise when on that particular morning I stumbled upon Alfie.

He was sitting by the edge of the lake that butted up against a steep incline of dirt and rock. Directly above him, maybe twenty feet up, was an old utility road that no one really used anymore except for park rangers. Alfie was fishing with a rod that looked like my dad's; it was not a child's toy. I half expected him to be smoking Camels and sipping from a can of beer, but he wasn't. He had his tackle box and lunch pail and a transistor radio that he was listening to through a small earplug.

Before he noticed me, there was the sound of a car coming to a stop up above. A car door opened. Boot-heavy feet shuffled for a moment and then something heavy hit the water maybe fifteen yards out. The car door slammed shut and there was the sound of rubber peeling out. It became obvious to Alfie that whatever was in that burlap sack now floating tenuously on the water's surface was alive. He dropped his pole, flung his transistor radio by the tackle box, dove into the water, and swam out to retrieve the sack. He carried it gingerly in his arms back to shore. I could hear from where I was crouching what sounded like the meowing of kittens. And sure enough, Alfie fished out of that sack four soaking kittens, each one clinging to him for dear life.

It struck me as odd, seeing Alfie holding these kittens in his arms and drying them off and calming their little palpitating hearts and making little faces at them as they licked his nose. Suddenly, he noticed me staring at him and gave me the merest hint of a smile. It was then, at the tender age of six, that I realized even a tattoo penetrates only a layer or two of the human hide. The rest of us is hidden and secret and not easily exposed or even shared. It takes moments like the one I shared secretly with Alfie—unrehearsed and unguarded—to get under the skin of things and to the truth. For none of us is as we appear.

I made my way back to my brothers, exhilarated and a little exhausted. It felt as if I had traveled a great distance in a very short period of time. I never told my brothers what I had witnessed. I never brought it up with Alfie either. But I'll tell you something I know is true: That early morning we became brothers, Alfie and I. And like all brothers, we let that little miracle at dawn pass by us unspoken, satisfied that merely basking in its light was sufficient, a silent prayer of praise and thanksgiving meant for the ears of a God who is not indifferent to the muffled cries of little kittens and other living things.

The City Prays

One early morning several years ago, I saw a city pray. An actual city. An entire city. Bricks and mortar, street lights and pavement, patches of dewy, sloping grass and trees laden with morning mist, streetcars and cable cars, bikes and buses. Oh, yes, and people too. Most importantly, the people of the city prayed. It was as if I were sitting on a bench with Walt Whitman and Carl Sandburg and Thomas Merton, the three of them there with eyes wide open and their mouths agape, vying for my attention with their own particular slant on what they were seeing.

Whitman whispered: "A million people—manners free and superb—open voices—hospitality—the most courageous and friendly young men. City of hurried and sparkling waters! City of spires and masts! City nested in bays! My city!"

Sandburg whispered: "Come and show me another city with lifted head singing so proud to be alive and coarse and strong and cunning. Flinging magnetic curses amid the toil of piling job on job; here is a tall bold slugger set vivid against the little soft cities."

Merton whispered: "As long as I am content to know that [God] is infinitely greater than I, and that I cannot know Him unless He shows Himself to me, I will have Peace, and He will be near me and in me, and I will rest in Him."

There I sat once on a park bench in San Francisco at dawn with two poets and a priest. I had dropped my mother off at the airport, she off to Medjugorje, insistent and defiant. She was *not* going to bend the ear of Mother Mary and ask that the insidious cancer slowly stifling the breath of her lungs might leave her, and I believed her. I recalled that morning Saint Monica, the sainted mother of the prodigal, sainted son Augustine, a woman who never stopped praying that God might make Himself known to her son and so save him from himself, the son who once boldly prayed, "LORD, make me chaste, but not yet!" And I realized that my mother was much like her fourth-century namesake, that she was a woman to whom God had made Himself known and who so rested in His embrace of Peace that she feared no one or no thing, not even cancer or dying.

> MY MOTHER FEARED NO ONE OR NO THING, NOT EVEN CANCER OR DYING.

I was sitting in Washington Square off Columbus Avenue, a stone's throw from Fisherman's Wharf. Lit on Telegraph Hill above me was Coit Tower, a monument built in memory of Lillie Hitchcock Coit, a beloved San Francisco socialite. Legend has it that one afternoon on her way home from school teenaged Lillie came upon short-staffed Engine Company No. 5 of the Volunteer Fire Department pulling its engines up Telegraph Hill to reach a fire. Remembering a childhood experience when she almost died in a fire, Lillie tossed her schoolbooks aside and rallied some male bystanders to help as she herself began hauling on the tow rope and shouting, "Come on, you men, pull!" No. 5 raced up the hill and was the first engine to douse the fire.

After that, Lillie became the mascot of No. 5, wearing an honorary uniform, smoking cigars, and playing poker with the men all night. She proudly sported a diamond-studded gold fireman's badge reading "No. 5," awarded her in 1863. Lillie was buried with that badge. Ah, Lillie, one of the first celebrated cross-dressers in San Francisco's storied and *avant-garde* history!

Across the square is Sts. Peter and Paul Catholic Church, with whitewashed Whitman spires reaching almost two hundred feet into the sky. A ribbon of verse from Dante's *Paradiso* dresses the façade: "The glory of Him who moves all things penetrates and glows throughout the universe." I had come to that square and that bench because I was having a hard time believing in the glory of the One who moves all things and penetrates and glows throughout the universe. I came because I was weary of searching for God in the tangle of air tubes and feeding tubes and pill bottles and cotton swabs and cancer coughs. I came so God might make Himself known to me. Alone in the square at the break of dawn, the Spirit prayed for me, for I was out of words: My heart is ready, O God, my heart is ready. Awake my soul; I will awake the dawn. I was ready, and I was awake. But was God awake? Was God ready? O God, arise above the heavens; may your glory shine on earth!

I needed to know that God was a part of it all, that God did not shy away from the sufferings of my mother, and that He stood by her as surely as He stood by His son on the cross. I needed to know that God could make His home—that His glory could shine—even in the shadow of my mother's misery, made tolerable only by her Christian faith and hope. I came with insistence and defiance equal to my mother's.

I WASN'T ASKING FOR A MIRACLE, THOUGH I SURELY WOULD HAVE TAKEN IT HAD IT BEEN PROFFERED.

I wasn't asking for a miracle, though I surely would have taken it had it been proffered. No, I plopped myself down in an open space in the middle of a city still asleep so that God might make Himself known *to me*.

I did not pray alone. For in the way that only a city can, San Francisco slowly opened her eyes and stretched her arms and shook the sleep from her legs and began to slowly rise from slumber. In the way that only a city can, San Francisco began to pray. Six octogenarian Chinese women appeared out of nowhere and positioned themselves in the middle of the lawn and moved to the silent music of Tai Chi. Across the street a middle-aged man parked and locked his bike in front of a produce store. Before reaching into his pocket for the keys to the store, he caught a glimpse of the Chinese women enjoying a kind of holy synchronicity across the way, and he studied them for a while. A hint of peace and satisfaction washed across his face, as if these women had somehow reached into his body with their soft, enduring hands and smoothed out the aches and the pains of his heart.

Somewhere in the distance a cable car bell rang to signal the sun to do its rising, and as if on cue the streetlights began to dim. And then, after a while, the parrots that make their nests in the tall eucalyptus on the upper reaches of Telegraph Hill swept down like bombers on a raid, but with beauty and grace in the wake of their sweep. And now, in the light of that early morning, I could see the city pray—not only old Chinese ladies and shopkeepers, but men in suits sipping Starbucks coffee and old Italian women in morning frocks sweeping off their stoops and backpacked children barely scrubbed tilting in the direction of school and the stumbling drunk making his way, like a squirrel, to the secret place where his bottle is hidden. It was all unfolding before me, and it was beautiful, all of it.

My brother Jack once offered what I considered a lame excuse for not going to Mass very often. "The world," he said, "is my church." I am not sure his thinking is so lame after all, for there in Washington Square I felt the presence of God. He made Himself known to me in the undying spirit that seemed to touch and pervade everything and every person as he or she went about their morning routines and rituals. Saint Thomas Aquinas would have called it an experience of sanctifying grace, a moment in time when grace produces in the soul a likeness to God that infinitely transcends that which exists in the purely natural order.

Here in "the City," as it is referred to by the natives—all but destroyed in its childhood by the Great Earthquake of 1865 and again in 1868 and then completely leveled by the Great Earthquake and Fire of 1906—was incontrovertible evidence of

I DID NOT PRAY ALONE. FOR IN THE WAY THAT ONLY A CITY CAN, SAN FRANCISCO SLOWLY OPENED HER EYES AND STRETCHED HER ARMS AND SHOOK THE SLEEP FROM HER LEGS AND BEGAN TO SLOWLY RISE FROM SLUMBER.

47

a divine spark that animates every soul and does not know death. Souls may suffer and they do; souls may be beaten down and know the sting of defeat, but they never die. I remembered the definition of faith given to the earliest followers of Jesus in the Letter to the Hebrews: Faith is the substance of things hoped for, the evidence of things not seen. With eyes of faith, I saw the City pray that morning, a city confident and calm and brimming over with hope, proud to be alive, unconcerned with things over which it had no control, aware of its past glories and humbling defeats but not beholden to them, a city forever young and daring like Lillie Hitchcock Coit and the old Chinese ladies and the man on the bike.

It was human imagination and human genius and human daring—gifts from a gracious God—that first created this city, and human sweat and human toil and human know-how that built, rebuilt, and rebuilt again every building of wood and brick and stone and paved the streets and laid the pipes and strung the wires—all in fitting tribute to a God whose glory penetrates all things and glows throughout the universe. At dawn the City prayed a morning prayer of praise to God, when I could not.

Prime
Six in the Morning
Work

You have made the moon to mark the seasons;

the sun knows its time for setting.

You make darkness, and it is night,

when all the animals of the forest come creeping out.

The young lions roar for their prey, seeking their food from God.

When the sun rises, they withdraw and lie down in their dens.

People go out to their work and to their labor until the evening.

Psalm 104

I Working in Eden

There is a town in the desert region of southern California called Mecca. It's tucked away among the vast orchards of grapefruit and dates and oranges that fuel the economy of the Coachella Valley. To the south rise the Santa Rosa Mountains, to the east the Little San Bernardino Mountains; and to the west flows a little trickle of a river, the San Felipe, lazily weaving its way over beds of dry earth on its way to the Gulf of California.

Mecca, at least when I was there twenty-five years ago, was a tired old town, beaten down by the desert sun, thirsting for the refreshing spring rains that came only occasionally from beyond the mountains that have stood guard over the town through the millennia.

> I KNEW I NEEDED A CHANGE AND A CHALLENGE.

Downtown Mecca had, by my recollection, four or five taverns, a bowling alley, a small market, a medical clinic that operated out of an old Quonset hut, and a gas station. Just outside of town was a small grapefruit grove and packing plant where I worked the summer after my sophomore year in college.

Earlier that year, I had decided I wanted to move on from my rather successful career flipping burgers at McDonald's and try something new. As much as I enjoyed sweating with pride over the grill and the deep fryers and at day's end scrubbing my body clean of the grease and the smell of Big Mac sauce that never really left me, I knew I needed a change and a challenge. So I joined six other University of Portland students and traveled to the desert where, we were assured by the Holy Cross priest who accompanied us, we would easily find jobs. A friend and I spent the first week picking green beans with migrant workers who secretly laughed at our white, soft, city bodies. We were paid fifty cents for every bushel we filled with beans. It was backbreaking work. One week and three encounters with rattlesnakes later, I moved on to another job, with deep respect for every single migrant worker in the world.

When it dawned on me, however, that I would be packing grapefruit from six in the morning until two in the afternoon in a poorly-ventilated warehouse in hellish heat punctured only occasionally by a fickle ceiling fan, I accepted the fact that this was going to be more of a lateral career move, not the upwardly destined one I had anticipated when I turned in my golden-arched uniform.

We rose before dawn to hundred-degree heat that percolated under the asphalt. Hazy steam rose from the sidewalks and streets, creating a dreamy image of buildings and trees and people off in the distance. In sleepy silence we sat at the kitchen table and devoured our scrambled eggs and refried beans and tortillas. Johnny and Alicia, our gracious hosts, kept the radio *and* the television tuned to sweet-talking dueling evangelists, who kept reminding us of the fires and torments of hell. "I bet he's never been to Mecca," my friend Mike grumbled once under his breath.

We arrived at the packing plant a little before six every workday morning. We climbed out of the flat bed of the old beat up Ford pickup and made our way to the break room. My memories are rich of that paradise in the desert, for that is what it turned out to be, at least for me. There among the cardboard boxes, the endless stream of grapefruit, the industrial strength coffee machine, the sound of the forklift loading packed boxes onto trucks, the radio serenading us with mariachi music, the laughter, the gossip and chatter, the foreman's menacing bark, we worked hard and efficiently, for we were paid seventeen cents a box. In a good hour, when the grapefruit were large and boxes required fewer of them, we often made twelve or thirteen dollars—a king's ransom to a retired McDonald's "associate" in 1979.

> ALL THE LINES THAT USUALLY DIVIDE US WERE ERASED. WE WERE AS GOD HAD CREATED US: FELLOW HUMAN BEINGS ENJOYING PARADISE.

When the town's air-raid horn sounded at noon, within seconds machines were reduced to silence and we were lounging around the shaded loading dock. Resting against boxes or wooden posts, we sat quietly and consumed our identical lunches: big, juicy grapefruits, usually two each. They were peeled without effort; the juice dripped down our fingers and hands. Biting into them, we had to conclude that somehow, mysteriously, they had been picked from the tree in the middle of the Garden of Eden. I would recline there eating my grapefruit, the red bandana around my head soaked in sweat, one moment looking out onto the rows and rows of ripe trees and another moment surveying the loading dock. Jamie and Laurie were to the left and right of Maureen, each one's head resting on one of her shoulders. Mike was reading a Faulkner novel; Lucita was breast-feeding her little baby boy. And Eleanor, my favorite and a grandmother of three, who owned the most colorful, gritty and earthy vocabulary in two languages west of the Mississippi, was wiping her brow, drinking a bottle of Pepsi through a straw, and resting her tired bones on a creaky old folding chair. These grapefruit we ate, picked from the Tree of Life sent to us directly from the Garden of Eden, had the most amazing effect on us. We were no longer men and women, Anglo and Latino, rich and poor, educated and unlearned. All the lines that usually divide us were erased. We were as God had created us: fellow human beings enjoying paradise.

During those moments of peace and quiet, with weary workers drinking in the warm, welcomed breeze, with grapefruit juice dripping down our chins, I knew what it was like before the Fall, before Adam and Eve were kicked out of Eden. I knew what it was like when all was peaceful and right and good, when no one hurt another or conspired in secret, when boundaries and borders did not exist and did not need to be guarded by guns, when grace and not greed got the heart beating faster, when the power of love and not the love of power electrified the earth. For a half hour each Monday through Friday that summer on the loading dock, I rested in paradise, a garden where dreams are born and never die, where hopes are nourished and the weary heart of the worker can rest, where we get a glimpse of how good we really can be when we take the risk to try.

The Spirit once led Jesus to the desert, to the place where hearts are won and lost.

the place where choices are made, where all of us, like our spiritual ancestors, toil

for the bread we eat and work the soil from which we came. After forty days of spir-

itual toil, angels came to minister to Jesus. And so they come from time to time to all

of us—we who labor till evening falls, doing work that is holy and good and fruitful

not because it makes us wealthy or famous or powerful but because it creates some-

thing good for our families, our neighbors, our town, our country, our world. If you believe this, if you believe that there is a divine nobility

EVEN SWEAT WRUNG FROM A DAY'S LABOR IS A PRAYER TO THE CREATOR, SPOKEN GRATEFULLY AND HUMBLY BY ANYONE WHO KNOWS THAT EVEN IN DESERT SOIL THE FRUIT OF PARADISE CAN GROW.

and grace bestowed upon all work (however humble or exalted) that creates some-

thing good, then you can understand how even sweat wrung from a day's labor is a

prayer to the Creator, spoken gratefully and humbly by anyone who knows that even

in desert soil the fruit of paradise can grow.

Breakfast with God

On the corner of NW Broadway and Everett in downtown Portland, there is a greasy-spoon restaurant called John's Café. I call it Police Headquarters, because on any given morning you can find at least five or six cops at the counter mopping their eggs up with dry toast and washing them down with around five cups of coffee each. From seven until ten in the morning, Monday through Friday, John's Café is the safest square block in the tri-county area. Back in the 1990s, it was run by an old Greek immigrant, his wife, and their eighteen-year-old grandson, who acted as dishwasher, busboy and interpreter. It was the kind of café your doctor warns you about, but I still loved it. The service was good; the ambience was vintage sixties; they cooked my eggs just the way I liked them. In the Hannon family, that is just about as good as life gets.

So when one day Peter Curtain asked me if I wanted to take him out for breakfast, John's Café was the first place I thought of. And for the next two years, on the first Monday of each month, Peter and I would have breakfast together at John's Café. It became our haunt. We would meet at Saint Vincent de Paul Church where I worked and together walk the five blocks to John's. Rain or shine. Always arriving with some amount of fanfare and fuss, we would sit in the same booth, the one closest to the bathrooms. Peter, being a rather large, loquacious man, would enter with cheerfulness dripping off him like water, saying hello to everyone, patting the shoulders of all the cops who, after the fourth or fifth time this occurred, rightfully concluded that Peter was harmless and refrained from instinctively reaching for their side arms. He would blow a kiss to Sylvia, the grandmother stationed behind the counter, and wave to her husband slinging hash at the grill. I half-enjoyed the spectacle, respectful of the fact that in the midst of all the hustle and bustle, this had become Peter's home base. He was like Norm Peterson in

IT WAS GRAND THEATRE, AND I LOVED IT.

"Cheers." Folks like Peter gravitate to watering holes and eateries like John's Café because it is a place where "everybody knows your name."

Placing our order at John's was like celebrating the old Latin Mass: a ritual wrapped in mystery and awe, lost to all but a very few who were privy to its inner workings. Peter had to have coffee from a fresh pot. It had to be poured into a mug that was free of chips or stains. His eggs had to be cooked over easy, with the stress on "easy." The toast had to have just come out of the toaster. The pieces had to be cut diagonally and placed around the plate. Hash browns had to be brown, not yellow. I know all this because that is how Peter ordered: He was specific and unapologetic, and he ordered each time as if it were the first time he had set foot in John's Café. It was grand theatre, and I loved it.

One Monday, Peter seemed sullen and unlike himself. He didn't kid me about my age, reminding me that he would always be one year older than I. He didn't call me "bucko" and mess up my hair or ask me what I thought of his new shoes (which I always said were the cat's meow, and that always made him laugh). There was none of the usual playful banter as we walked from the church to John's Café. And when we arrived, there was no patting the cops on the back, no blowing a kiss to grandma, no saying howdy to the cook. Peter sat across from me and fished out four or five prescription bottles from various pockets. He counted out his medication and placed the pills on the table as he always did. Without those pills, Peter would be languishing in a state hospital somewhere counting the ceiling tiles instead of being here where he needed to be, blended into the soup of humanity.

Our breakfast arrived, and I dug right in, leaving Peter in the dust, nibbling his toast like a mouse and sipping his coffee. Only the clinking of forks and knives saved us from complete silence. Then Peter looked up at me and gazed straight into my eyes as if to say: Listen, I know that a lot of the time you humor me because I'm mentally ill and that I usually ask questions that have no real basis in reality, but I want an honest answer to this question, okay?

"Fr. Pat, does God love me?" he asked.

God only knows from what dark recess of doubt or hurt or fear or anxiety this question came, but I knew Peter was genuine in his concern, that he had been pondering this question for a very, very long time. I gave him the only answer I had: "Yes, Peter. God loves you." (More than you will ever know, I thought to myself.) Peter was obviously relieved by the answer, because a huge grin appeared on his face and his appetite returned with a vengeance.

Five minutes later, however, Peter was down again, finger painting with his egg yolks, scratching his head nervously. Again he looked up at me and asked, "Fr. Pat, does God love me?" To which I responded, this time with my hand on his arm, "Yes,

> GOD SEES US FOR WHO WE TRULY ARE AND LOVES US WITHOUT ASKING FOR ANY-THING IN RETURN.

Peter, you know God loves you." Once again the fog lifted, the sun shone brightly, and all was well with the world. But soon Peter's chin was scraping the ground again, his spirits siphoned out of him, his heart broken. Isn't this just like the rest of us, I thought. We're down, we're up, and we're down again. Peter looked up at me, this time with tears coming out of his eyes. He looked like a child lost at a carnival, surrounded by a throng of people yet so very alone. "Fr. Pat," he asked me a third time, "does God love me?" Well, it finally dawned on me that something mysterious was going on here, that together Peter and I had stepped into something quite sacred. John's Café had, under our very noses, become holy ground.

Taking Peter's hands into mine, I looked into his eyes and said, "Peter, you know you have asked me this question three times now. I think you know the answer. I want you to go to the peaceful place in the deepest part of your heart where Jesus lives. Go there and stay there for a few minutes. Then I'm going to ask *you* a question." Peter agreed. We sat there for four or five minutes. I gazed out the window, finished my orange juice, listened in on the conversation in the booth adjacent to ours, and planned out the rest of my morning. Then looking at Peter and once again taking his hands into mine, I asked him, "Peter, does God love you?" Peter paused a moment, freed up one of his hands to take a sip from his coffee, and then with a tone of truth in his voice I have never heard before or since said, "You know, Fr. Pat, I'm optimistic."

I have since come to believe that there is no greater confession of faith than the one Peter uttered that Monday morning at John's Café in Portland, Oregon. A wounded, broken man went on a journey into himself and discovered that perhaps he was not alone, that in the very shadow of his heart he might find the God who loved him. He was optimistic. How great is *that?*

I have also come to believe that John's Café and similar gathering places are like churches, places where police officers and immigrant cooks and their wives and children and priests and folks like Peter can leave their aloneness at the door and step into a warm and welcoming place where everyone knows their name.

God sees us for who we truly are and loves us without asking for anything in return. This I had forgotten and was reminded of one Monday morning by a man whose mind is often lost in a fog but whose heart optimistically holds a lovely and beautiful dwelling place for that same God.

III — *A Soul Kissed by God*

Margaret Delaney lives in a single-room-occupancy hotel in downtown Portland. Her legs are about half the normal length of a person her size, and they gave up on her completely when she was around twenty. In the intervening years, Margaret has gained a lot of weight; now at around forty, she must easily tip the scale at three hundred pounds. She gets around the city in an electric-powered wheelchair. You can always tell when she is coming even before you see her, because the noise from her motorized chair gives her away. To tell the truth, most folks appreciate the warning, because Margaret is pretty ugly by Hollywood standards. Her long, black, stringy hair collapses dead upon her shoulders. She wears thick glasses that make her deep blue eyes appear twice their size. Her denim overalls drape over her like a tent, and they always have crumbs and Diet Coke stains on them. Her teeth are pretty well gone now, and her Converse high tops flap free of shoelaces. Margaret Delaney is quite an unsightly sight.

I first met Margaret when she sped her way up the main aisle of the Downtown Chapel for Communion one morning, the first week I arrived as the new associate. I do not think she had bathed in many weeks, because the closer she got the more pungent the odor became. Then there she was, right before me, her big eyes staring at me.

"The Body of Christ," I said, my eyes beginning to water.

"AMEN!" Margaret yelled in a deep, husky voice. Then she stuck out her tongue, keeping her blue eyes trained on mine, almost daring me to look the other way. By the grace of God I didn't, and I think by that very non-act I won Margaret Delaney's heart.

Some days I'd be at a coffee shop or a bookstore reading the paper in the morning and she would see me through the window and wave at me. I'd wave back. And then she would negotiate her way through the door of the shop or store, bump tables, run over feet, and make her way to my table. I would look around and see folks with frozen, horrified looks on their faces as she passed them. No one would say anything, of course, at least nothing louder than a whisper. Mostly they just looked away, gobbled up the last of their food, and headed out the door. Margaret would sit there with me, gaze upon me with her laser eyes, and dare me to look away. I would try not to, because something inside of me told me God was trying to teach me something and I'd better pay attention.

"SO, WHAT'S GOING ON?" Margaret would begin. I had learned that her normal, matter-of-fact voice was in fact a shout.

I'd respond, "Oh, not much. How are you, Margaret?"

And she would always say the same thing every time: "I'M DOING GREAT, FR. PAT. THANK YOU VERY MUCH."

Then we'd talk about her cat, the hassles of wheelchair repair, and the weather. After a while Margaret would swing around, give me a thumbs up, and maneuver her way out of the store, yelling behind her, "I'LL SEE YOU IN CHURCH!"

And I always did, for church was where Margaret did her best work.

Margaret Delaney was our most dependable lector. She read the Scriptures at Mass in a way that made you say to yourself, "This lady really believes what she is reading." She was also a minister of the Eucharist. It was a blessing to be in her line to receive the Precious Blood, because you understood in the very depth of your soul as you took the cup from Margaret's grimy hands and pressed it against your lips that it truly was the Blood of Christ—shed for the forgiveness of our sins and the healing of the world. After Communion, as the closing hymn was being sung, Margaret would zoom around the church so she could hand out the Sunday bulletins to the parishioners. Before Palm Sunday, it was Margaret who took the bundles of palm fronds and did the painstaking job of separating them. She was a fixture at the church and took her work very seriously. Stripped of the means to do anything else, Margaret tilled the soil of the vineyard that was the Downtown Chapel of Saint Vincent de Paul on the corner of Sixth and Burnside.

One day I visited Margaret in her apartment. Her wheelchair was in the shop for repairs, so I had come by to give her Communion. Her apartment was a disaster area. Pots and pans were stacked in the sink; piles of dirty clothes congregated in every corner; a thick layer of dust and crumbs covered most everything. She offered me a bowl of Cap'n Crunch cereal, which I accepted, and we sat there talking about her cat, the hassles of wheelchair repair, and the weather.

After I had given her Communion, her phone rang. While she was talking on the phone, I let my eyes wander and was amazed at what they finally rested upon. On the wall in front of me were two framed pictures. On the left was a picture of a beautiful young girl, maybe eight or nine years old. She had on a delicate, white-laced dress and a white veil. Her hands were pressed together in front of her, and her eyes were a deep

and penetrating blue. Next to what most certainly was Margaret's First Communion picture hung a picture of Jesus and his most Sacred Heart. You know, the kind you see on
pious holy cards. Only then did it begin to dawn on me who Margaret Delaney really
was. Underneath the dirty denim, beneath the thin layer of unwashed skin, behind the
thick glasses, inside the floppy Converse high tops was one of God's most precious cre-
ations.

There is an old Norwegian myth about heaven. As the story goes, before a baby is
born, God takes its soul into His hands, and before that soul is released and given flesh
and blood and bone as a home, God takes
that soul and kisses it with great tenderness.
Though the baby may not remember the
kiss, God does. Even if we cannot see the
impression of God's lips on our souls, God can.

> CHURCH WAS WHERE
> MARGARET DID HER
> BEST WORK.

Margaret must have remembered somehow that God kissed her soul before she was
born, because that memory must have seen her through the long and lonely nights
when her body began to betray her, when over time her voice hardened and her beauty faded. The memory of that kiss must have been a faithful companion when everyone
else—myself included—began to hold their noses, catch their breaths, look the other
way, and leave her behind. The memory of that kiss must have brought her back to the
only table where bread is always broken and shared with every living soul, where the
cup is poured out willingly and without care or concern for whose lips press against it.
And the memory of that kiss must have given Margaret her life's work: to proclaim the

word of God, to minister at the table, and on occasion to bump her wheelchair into the oncoming lives of folks who would otherwise step aside.

Like the leper who had the courage to come before the Master and say matter-of-factly, "You can cure me if you really want to," Margaret approached the Communion table with that same confidence.

No one wants to feel as if he or she doesn't count. No one wants to be thrown out, cast away, or pushed aside. To be fully human is to feel a part of the family. One day Margaret Delaney must have cried out to Jesus, "If you really want to, you can heal me." And Jesus surely replied, "I do want to. Be cured." And that day Margaret lifted her lifeless legs out of bed and hoisted herself into her wheelchair and made her way to church.

TO BE FULLY HUMAN IS TO FEEL A PART OF THE FAMILY.

Dorothy Day once said, "No one has the right to feel hopeless. There is too much work to do." Margaret Delaney believed this in her gut because she knew she was more than just her body. She belonged; she was loved; her work had meaning and significance. For she remembered and remembers still, I hope, what the leper must have remembered and what too many of us forget: Before we were born, our souls were kissed by God.

CHAPTER FOUR

Terce
Nine in the Morning
The Holy Spirit

Where can I go from your spirit? Or where can I flee from your presence?

If I ascend to heaven, you are there; if I make my bed in Sheol, you are there.

If I take the wings of the morning and settle at the farthest limits of the sea,

even there your hand shall lead me, and your right hand shall hold me fast.

If I say, "Surely the darkness shall cover me, and the light around me become night,"

even the darkness is not dark to you; the night is as bright as the day,

for darkness is as light to you.

Psalm 139

I *Intoxication*

Nicky Drabec and Glen Bonora were bounced out into the playground like drunkards tossed from the neighborhood tavern, except in this case the bouncer wore a black habit, smelled of talcum, and went by the name Sr. Delfina. It was the first day of fifth grade, and Nick and Glen had broken the all-school record for the quickest detentions ever received. It was a record that would hold for three years, that is until Nick, God only knows how, managed to get himself a detention in August, a full three weeks before the start of the new term.

He and Glen had sneaked into the school at the behest of their classmates in order to chase down the tantalizing rumor that we were going to have a new teacher. Sr. Virgenmina, a nun whose reputation for severe discipline and lightning quick reflexes with a ruler earned her the nickname "Sr. Virgenmeany," had taught fifth grade since the dawn of humanity (as far as any of us was concerned) at Our Lady of Grace Catholic School. Nick and Glen emerged from the school with the news that Sr. Virgenmina would be teaching seventh grade this year, but they couldn't tell us who our new teacher was going to be. Bets were placed and the early favorite was Sr. Anna Maria, our beloved second-grade teacher, who regularly stole bikes from the bike rack to ride like a demon during recess, black habit and veil blowing in the wind.

The morning bell finally rang, and we all filed into our classroom. And there she was, Miss Kathy Walsh, twenty-three years old, freshly minted from teacher's school, standing at the front of class, welcoming her brood for the first time. The absence of the dark Carmelite habit took us all by surprise. Since first grade, every teacher we had was a nun. None of us quite knew how to react to having a teacher with hair and makeup and high heels. Some of us instinctively said, "Good morning, Sister," as we made our way to our desks. I was transfixed. I

> THE ABSENCE OF THE DARK CARMELITE HABIT TOOK US ALL BY SURPRISE.

somehow managed to place my lunch and coat in the closet in the back of the classroom and make it to my desk without taking my eyes off this vision of beauty. I sat there the whole day, and I don't remember anything she actually said. I just remember her silky voice and her green eyes and the dimples that appeared when she smiled.

After lunch Miss Walsh was putting us through our first spelling drill. She was pacing the room quickly, barking out words, letting us know she meant business. When she passed by my desk I felt the softest of breezes pass with her and with it the sweet smell of perfume that left me intoxicated and dizzy. By the end of the day, I had a full-blown crush on my fifth-grade teacher.

Before the final bell rang, I remember looking around the class and noticing the most remarkable thing. All the girls were acting like they normally did (which to us boys seemed annoyingly good). But observing the boys was like stepping through the looking glass to Opposite Land. For four years we boys had carefully cultivated our reputation as the most unruly, irreverent, surly, obnoxious gang of potential delinquents in the school. But looking at the class that day, you would have seen twenty-two boys sitting straight up at their desks, listening to Miss Walsh, responding quickly and with great enthusiasm, smiling with boyish embarrassment at her compliments. Hair stayed combed, shirts tucked in, shoelaces knotted, faces scrubbed, shoes spit-shined. Had the other boys felt the breeze too? Had they taken in the scent of her perfume and become drunk with joy as I had? All of our faces and ears were red with awkward bashfulness, a visible sign of a fire that had been stoked in our hearts and was now burning out of control, leaving in its wake the empty shells of our former selves.

The days and weeks that followed confirmed what I imagine we all suspected. Little fires blazed in little male hearts that quickened in her presence, and she changed us. Richard Salas, who had not spoken a word since first grade, became a chatterbox. You couldn't pay him to stop talking. Nick and Glen stopped collecting detention slips like baseball cards and assumed a more dignified posture in class. Boys who would normally be hightailing it out of the classroom at day's end were

> BY THE END OF THE DAY, I HAD A FULL-BLOWN CRUSH ON MY FIFTH-GRADE TEACHER.

staying behind to clean the blackboard and pound out the erasers. Class clowns saved their best stuff for recess, bowing without as much as a fight to Miss Walsh's suggestion that they behave. Wallflowers blossomed. Bullies repented and retired, healing the runts of the classroom litter of their nervous ticks and flinches. I don't think a single serious punishment was handed out that year to a fifth-grade boy. All because we boys were caught in the wake of a perfumed breeze that left us on fire with a kind of love we can name only now with any real authority.

> IN EFFECTING THIS MOST UNLIKELY TRANSFORMATION, LOVE OFFERED CLEAR EVIDENCE OF ITS POWER.

It was, in a way, our first real Pentecost experience, for it followed the same script of that ancient day when a group of frightened disciples, huddled in a darkened room, found themselves caught in the wake of a most powerful breeze, leaving their hearts on fire with love. It was a breeze that came without warning or whisper but left them upside down, inside out, and completely turned around. No one has ever seen the Holy Spirit, but as with the wind that rustles the leaves on a tree, we can point to its effect. For a group of fifth-grade boys in 1970, a faintly perfumed breeze tamed the tiger in us and made us into a pretty decent group of kids. And in effecting this most unlikely transformation, love offered clear evidence of its power.

II *Running into the Arms of God*

When we were kids, my brothers and sisters and I loved it when Dad got that wistful, sentimental look in his eye. He would be sitting in his big green-leather overstuffed chair on a Saturday evening, let's say, listening to Sinatra on the stereo or watching Lawrence Welk on the television. We kids would pick up the scent pretty quickly, for we knew that when Dad was in a mellow mood he handed over his money to us with a minimum of pleading on our part. We jackals would pounce on our prey, leaving a pile of penniless bones behind. Dad never knew what hit him.

I was the odd child of the brood: I rarely asked for money. Instead, I asked for stories. Dad wasn't much of a talker, so it was only while he was being relieved of his weekly earnings that he would tell me stories about his father and mother and grandparents. The one he liked to retell most was how his grandfather got to California. Other Golden State families can trace their forebears to the Gold Rush or to those early pioneers who braved raging waters and the Rockies in covered wagons to attain the rich earth of the Central Valley. Still others could claim the early Spanish settlers as their progenitors. And a rare few could claim the honor of having an ancient Native American chief or warrior or shaman as their ancestor. We Hannons, however, take a certain amount of pride in the fact that our great-grandfather, Charles Krumlinde, arrived in California one day as a seventeen-year-old sailor on a Prussian navy vessel. It had docked a few miles south of Half Moon Bay, a small seaport town down the coast from San Francisco, in the fall of 1870. When the ship set sail, the kid from a small farming village near Hamburg went AWOL and stayed behind. He became a farmer, married a beautiful Irish lass named Mary Barry, and with her raised six children. One of them was my grandmother, my father's mother.

Since then our family has steered clear of the "dishonorable discharge" that marked our beginnings and can happily claim not a single felon among us. In fact, Charles' bloodline ironically produced nine lawyers in the last two generations alone, as well as several civil servants, a smattering of teachers, one archbishop, and one priest—me. Life all evens out in the end.

I conjure up the memory of my mutinous great-grandfather Charles because his humble beginnings mirror most of ours. When I ponder the action of God in my life and in the lives of others, I think it is important to be clear about the mixed bag God has to work with. None of us stands before God unsullied, and certain portions of our memories are best left

> I RARELY ASKED FOR MONEY.
> INSTEAD, I ASKED FOR STORIES.

locked and hidden. But God's Spirit moves where it wills. It is breath that fills our tired lungs, the wind beneath our weary wings, a gentle breeze that refreshes us, and the occasional storm that pushes us where we would never go on our own. And it is everywhere, a fitting reminder that not even our hidden past is an obstacle to God.

Mindful that we are being chased, we have to admit that most of the time we run away from the Holy Spirit. I guess such an instinct for survival is not totally irrational, because we know deep down what the Holy Spirit can do to us if it gets hold of our hearts. It strips away all our defenses. It tears down our carefully constructed walls and leaves us exposed, naked and vulnerable. Given a choice between courage and caution, miracles and mediocrity, too often we choose the safer path—out of fear, if nothing else. And so we run, like our ancestors. We run until we are too tired to run. We collapse in an upper room, lock the doors and bar the windows, and huddle together like trapped mice.

But what we think is the end of the story is only the beginning. For locked doors, barred windows, and frightened hearts are not obstacles to God's free and loving Spirit. Someone once wrote: "Love is greater than hatred. Forgiveness is greater than sin. And God is ultimately greater than anything that opposes God." I recall those words every time I find myself cornered by fear or completely lost. God will always hunt us down, find us, and take our fear and our fright away.

One image I can offer of this persistent Spirit is that of my cousin Debbie. We spent one fateful summer together on our grandma's farm in Tulelake, California. I was six and puny; she was twelve and huge. I spent the greater part of my waking hours that summer running around the perimeter of the farmhouse from Debbie and her "juicy kisses," as she liked to call them. I would be shrieking in terror as she slowly wore me down, until at last I would collapse on the front lawn and lie there in surrender to her wet kisses on my red cheeks.

That is what the Holy Spirit does to us. It wears us down until we can't run anymore. And then we are blessed with a kiss. That moment of helpless embrace, of sweet surrender is, believe me, a prayer.

CHAPTER FIVE

Sext: Noontime Silence

You silence the roaring of the seas, the roaring of their waves, the tumult of the peoples.

Those who live at earth's farthest bounds are awed by your signs;

you make the gateways of the morning and the evening shout for joy.

You visit the earth and water it, you greatly enrich it; the river of God is full of water;

you provide the people with grain, for so you have prepared it.

You water its furrows abundantly, settling its ridges, softening it with showers,

and blessing its growth.

You crown the year with your bounty; your wagon tracks overflow with richness.

The pastures of the wilderness overflow, the hills gird themselves with joy,

the meadows clothe themselves with flocks, the valleys deck themselves with grain,

they shout and sing together for joy.

Psalm 65

I Silent Soldiers

I was welcomed at birth into a family that thrived on chaos, encouraged conflict, and was viscerally suspicious of silence. If you were quiet for too long, it meant you were up to something.

This propensity for fighting, for arguing, for speaking loud and long, for transforming the symphonic into the cacophonous, must be a recessive gene in our family. To hear my mother tell it, her childhood was idyllic, peaceful, marked by obedience and reverence to all things living. (Yeah,

> IF YOU WERE QUIET FOR TOO LONG, IT MEANT YOU WERE UP TO SOMETHING.

right, my siblings and I would often mutter. We suspected this historical revisionism was mere propaganda, but Mom never strayed from the script.) Dad grew up on a farm, and all our research supported the conclusion that our paternal grandparents ran a pretty tight ship. We knew my dad was pretty good with his fists and with his hunting rifle, that he drove the pickup truck a little too fast and probably nipped a little whiskey in high school, but he was apparently an angel at home.

Early in her marriage, my mom had a conversation with my dad's mom that is instructive in this matter. Dad must have done something to upset my mother, so one afternoon Mom took it upon herself to confide in her mother-in-law certain things that irritated her about my father. My grandmother listened, and when my mother finished her lament, Grandma took a sip from her tea and said to her, "Well, I don't know about all that, but he was perfect when I gave him to you." I don't think she was kidding.

When we moved from our home on Arcadian Drive in 1971, just about every door in our house had to be replaced because one of the Hannon kids had kicked a hole in it or dented it with a shoe, a book, a shovel, or a younger sibling. We had built elaborate forts in the hallways, roller-derbied in the garage, and conducted wrestling matches in the living room. Every bedroom except our parents' was declared a disaster area. I used to take an occasional tour of my parents' bedroom and adjoining bathroom just to see how normal people lived.

I honestly don't know how my parents got any peace and quiet. The noise was bad enough when we were conscious and awake, but most of us even talked in our sleep. My folks had ten children in eleven years. As good Catholics they accepted each of us as God's gift, but they had to have known what they were getting themselves into. Thus the norm in our house became the kind of raucous revelry more commonly associated with Chicago city council sessions.

There was a game we used to play when we were kids, a little competition instigated by our parents. It was called "Dead Soldiers." It was quite simple. Mom or Dad would say, "Okay, let's play Dead Soldiers!" "Yay!" we would respond. And then the game would begin. If you made a sound, you lost. The last silent soldier standing won. On its face it was a preposterous, conniving little game. But we were kids who thrived on competition. My brother Mike, for example, once bet my brother Jack, recently gifted with a BB gun, that Jack couldn't hit him from fifty yards. Jack walked off the 150 feet in the street, turned, aimed, fired, and hit Mike in the fleshy part of his left leg. Mike dutifully handed over the buck he had wagered, and as he was rubbing his wound said, "Bet you can't hit me from seventy-five yards." Playing Dead Soldiers in our family was a piece of cake.

> ON ITS FACE IT WAS A PREPOSTEROUS, CONNIVING LITTLE GAME. BUT WE WERE KIDS WHO THRIVED ON COMPETITION.

We played Dead Soldiers mostly at dinnertime or on long drives in the car (one station wagon, two parents, nine kids; no kidding). When we were all relatively young, Dead Soldiers paid pretty healthy dividends for Mom and Dad. Sometimes they could get fifteen or twenty minutes of complete silence out of us. I wonder, in retrospect, what they were thinking about during those serene interludes. My hunch is that they weren't thinking about much at all. They were drinking in the silence, gulping it down like thirsty travelers girding themselves for a long desert crossing.

Of course, you don't have to have nine kids to know that silence is a rare commodity in our day and age. From the moment we awake to the moment we fall asleep, most of us are bombarded by noise of all kinds: the radio, the television, the telephone, the car engine and highway traffic, airplanes flying over, trains passing through, pedestrians with cell phones, the thump, thump, thump of the bass speakers in the tinted-window sports car idling next to us at the traffic stop. The purring engine of our culture lulls us into a kind of humming, hypnotic state where absolute silence is almost scary. Given all the modes of communication and transportation devised over the past hundred years to bring us closer together, one of the casualties has been our ability or desire—for lack of sustained silence—to listen.

> MY HUNCH IS THAT THEY WEREN'T THINKING ABOUT MUCH AT ALL. THEY WERE DRINKING IN THE SILENCE, GULPING IT DOWN LIKE THIRSTY TRAVELERS GIRDING THEMSELVES FOR A LONG DESERT CROSSING.

Prayer has as its starting point silence; for if we wish to listen to the voice of God we must first make silent the world around us. And as the psalmist reminds us, God will do His part: "You still the roaring of the seas, the roaring of their waves, and the tumult of the peoples." God will speak to us and tell us what we most need to hear. Such is the power of silence: In its wake is the voice of God.

Noted French composer Claude Debussy understood this when he said, "Music is the silence between the notes." I'm not much of a student of music, but even one unschooled in music theory can be struck by the truth of Debussy's observation. The pause, the silent moment is what makes music possible. As it is with a song or a symphonic piece, so it is with our lives. We can and must fill our lives with sounds of all sorts. What makes it music, however, are not these thousands of notes but the silence that sustains them.

Maybe there is—even in our day—such a thing as beautiful noise: the tinkling of the Salvation Army bell at Christmastime, the revving of a newly rebuilt engine, the crack of the wooden bat as it connects squarely with the ball, the infant's wail, the hum of conversation that hovers over a crowded restaurant, the train whistle from a long distance, the misplaced giggle at Mass. These sounds must be what the psalmist meant when he spoke of the earth cheering and singing for joy. But it is the pause between the notes, the silence behind the sound that makes the music. Silence is what, in the end, makes prayer possible.

So when we Hannon children played Dead Soldiers, our folks found the silence they needed to make sense of all that beautiful noise that filled their day. I'm sure it was a powerful moment of prayer for both of them, for that silence allowed them to hear the voice of God telling them how lucky and fortunate they were to have such amazing, talented and gifted children—God's gifts, each and every one of us.

CHAPTER SIX

None
Three in the Afternoon
Eucharist

The Lord is my shepherd, I shall not want.

He makes me lie down in green pastures;

He leads me beside still waters; he restores my soul.

He leads me in right paths for his name's sake.

Even though I walk through the darkest valley, I fear no evil;

for you are with me; your rod and your staff—they comfort me.

You prepare a table before me in the presence of my enemies;

you anoint my head with oil; my cup overflows.

Surely goodness and mercy shall follow me all the days of my life,

and I shall dwell in the house of the Lord my whole life long.

Psalm 23

I *A Portion of Bread, A Drop of Wine*

In a letter to a close friend, the great Catholic writer Flannery O'Connor recounts a conversation she had one evening while at dinner with friends: "I was once, five or six years ago, taken by some friends to have dinner with Mary McCarthy and her husband, Mr. Broadwater. She departed the Church at the age of fifteen and is now a Big Intellectual. We went at eight, and at one [in the morning] I hadn't opened my mouth once, there being nothing for me in such company to say.... Well, towards morning the conversation turned on the Eucharist, which I, being the Catholic, was obviously supposed to defend. Mrs. Broadwater said when she was a child and received the Host, she thought of it as the Holy Ghost, He being the 'most portable' person of the Trinity; now she thought of it as a symbol and implied that it was a pretty good one. I then said, in a very shaky voice, 'Well, if it's a symbol, to hell with it.' That was all the defense I was capable of, but I realize now that this is all I will ever be able to say about it...except that it is the center of existence for me; all the rest of life is expendable."

I can still remember to this day the September afternoon Fr. Stack gave my first-grade classmates and me a thorough tour of Our Lady of Grace Church in Castro Valley,

California, our first foray into the secret and hidden corridors of that massive building whose walls smelled of ancient incense, whose pews had been worn soft and smooth by years of use. He showed us the sacristy, where the wine was kept. (I can't help but think that several of my buddies made a mental note of the location for future consideration.) He pointed out the Stations of the Cross, the statues of Mary and Joseph, and the huge crucifix hanging behind the altar. He showed us the confessional boxes and how it all looked from where he sat. He let us walk around the sanctuary, touch the altar, sit one by one in the presider's chair. Finally, he brought us to the tabernacle, gold and glimmering, a befitting home for consecrated bread. Genuflecting before the tabernacle, Fr. Stack took a key and unlocked its front door. (I mention this only because Walt Stevens had asked Fr. Stack if the Lord's house had a back door too.) Sitting before Fr. Stack, our faces betraying a kind of awe, we waited silently as he turned toward us with a consecrated host held gently by the thumb and forefinger of his right hand. "This, my children," Fr. Stack uttered in a hushed tone signifying mystery and awe, "is the Body of Christ." To which we all responded in unison: "Ohhhhhhhh!"—a response that drew a faint smile from Fr. Stack. He had us right where he wanted us. "Now go to recess, children, and play fair," the venerable old priest said to us as he placed the host back in the tabernacle. The class broke out into spontaneous cheers and applause, much to the chagrin of our teacher Miss Sarti, because we were supposed to have math next. Walking out into the sunlight, Walt Stevens remarked, "Hey, we should visit church more often!"

A white wafer, no thicker than a playing card, becomes the Body of Christ. A cup of red wine, pressed from the fruit of the vine and almost too sweet to taste, becomes the Blood of Christ. So this is what brings old men and old women and their children and their children's children to their knees. Presidents and paupers, captains of industry and sixteen-year-old fast-food workers: When they come to the table for Eucharist, they are united by the same hunger, the same thirst. At the table we take a mere morsel of bread and the slightest sip of wine and admit there is a fundamental poverty and precariousness to life that, when genuinely embraced, helps bridge the divide that separates us, rich from poor, powerful from weak, young from old.

HE HAD US RIGHT WHERE HE WANTED US.

Years ago, when I worked at the downtown parish of Saint Vincent de Paul in Portland, there was one especially memorable weekday noon Mass. While we gathered around the altar during the Lord's Prayer, the president of the biggest bank in Portland held hands with Jean, an old homeless woman who had parked her shopping cart next to the statue of Saint Vincent, where she could keep her eye on it. It struck me then that Flannery O'Conner was right, that this meal we share has got to be more than just a symbol. Something far more powerful and mysterious is at play when fingers from separate hands—one manicured, the other mangled—are laced together in familial embrace at the table of Eucharist. Little by little, Eucharist works on us, often in secret, to soften our hearts and slowly, over time, fashion and form us into the image of God's beloved Son.

And like the last supper that Jesus shared with his disciples, the Eucharistic feast, the one that unites us despite it all, is eternal, unbeholden to the constraints of time and space and human limitations. Humbling it is to know that a portion of the bread and a drop of the wine are sufficient for all eternity.

Boxing Gloves

The last things Mom and Dad should have given my brother Brian for his fourteenth birthday were boxing gloves. But there they were: all shiny and black, two sets of untouched leather boxing gloves in a box with the words "Guaranteed to Last a Lifetime" scrolled across it like a death sentence. We all looked at each other in subdued horror, the brothers and sisters. All of us, that is, except Brian, who had the biggest grin I've ever seen on a living mammal. The ground shifted beneath us as the balance of power shifted even more toward the eldest of our clan. What were our parents thinking? Hadn't they picked up on the subtle hints we had given them that Brian was a cruel despot not to be trusted? How many times had they seen us standing at the living room window weeping as they drove off to dinner and a movie, having left us in the care of the adolescent equivalent of Jabba the Hutt, who saw us as mere vassals whose purpose in life was to keep him fed and comfortable? Had they already forgotten what had happened the previous Christmas when

> WHAT WERE OUR PARENTS THINKING? HADN'T THEY PICKED UP ON THE SUBTLE HINTS WE HAD GIVEN THEM THAT BRIAN WAS A CRUEL DESPOT NOT TO BE TRUSTED?

they bought him a BB gun and Brian managed to shoot Jack in the kneecap "accidentally" after Jack refused to let Brian ride his new bike? Now boxing gloves? Evidently, the forces of natural selection were at play in the Hannon household, and the youngest, most frail boy among us (me) did not expect to survive.

We kids were like nineteenth-century Europe, a collection of shifting alliances, motivated by self-interest and personal survival. Your ally today was your enemy tomorrow. On any given day, someone in the family was fighting with someone else. With an arsenal of swear words and ugly looks and bloody fists, we scrapped and scraped with each other over territorial claims, bathroom rights, television control, and personal property. Whatever wasn't bolted or nailed down (or physically sitting in Mom and Dad's room) was fair game for appropriation. But now disputes were to be settled with boxing gloves.

So by the summer of 1967, Brian pretty much owned the house. The last of the treaties had been signed. Jack moved in with Mike, Greg and me, and Brian now had his own bedroom. When Mom and Dad were gone, Brian had complete control of the television set. We kept him satisfied and appeased, knee-deep in peanut-butter-and-jelly sandwiches and Coca-Cola. And Brian used Jack's bike any time he darn well pleased. An uneasy peace settled upon 3635 Arcadian Drive.

One morning, however, while the rest of us were at school, Julie—all of three and half years old—waddled into the kitchen, boxing gloves gracing her delicate little hands. She climbed into the seat next to our mother, who was sipping her morning coffee and taking a crack at the crossword puzzle. Julie reared back and landed a punch that set my mother sprawling onto the Formica-tiled floor. "POW!" Julie screamed. Though we didn't know it then, Brian's days were numbered. The revolution had begun.

Brian's despotic reign ended that evening. Mom sat with us at the kitchen table, nursing her eye with a cold piece of rib-eye steak, listening to us as we stumbled over each other recounting the terms of our unconditional surrender to our eldest brother. She must have marveled at how well we had kept things hidden from her. Had she not that very day sung our praises to the butcher and the lady at the checkout stand at Romley's Market? Had she not beamed with maternal pride as the pharmacist at Carl's Drugs complimented her on her well-behaved and polite children? Had she not thumbed through the photo album

> JULIE REARED BACK AND LANDED A PUNCH THAT SET MY MOTHER SPRAWLING ONTO THE FORMICA-TILED FLOOR.

that very morning, shedding tears of thanksgiving upon the pictures of her nine children, only now to find out that most of the time we were at each other's throats?

We all climbed into the station wagon that next Sunday and went to Mass. I don't know for sure what my mother and father were praying for that morning as they knelt there in the pew, eyes closed, hands folded together, fingers laced tightly under their chins. The mystical Saint John had a vision all his own that must have come close to what my parents were praying for that morning: a new heaven and a new earth, a world of peace and reconciliation where wounds are healed, where the lost are found, where the weakest are protected, where there are no more tears. And my mother and father? I bet they entertained a vision of a home where their children got along most of the time, a home that nurtured a kind of loyal love that would in time become bedrock.

Somewhere in the backyard of 3635 Arcadian Drive, there is buried a box that contains two sets of leather boxing gloves that were guaranteed to last a lifetime. We don't know exactly where. Mom took that information with her to heaven. But their burial was an important one for us as a family. We still fought as brothers and sisters do. But we began to understand that day what I imagine all of us come to learn as

> ANY WEAPON, EVEN A SET OF KIDS' BOXING GLOVES, BRANDISHED BY AN ANGRY OR HATEFUL OR HURTING HEART CAN LAST A LIFETIME, IF WE LET IT.

followers of Jesus: Any weapon, even a set of kids' boxing gloves, brandished by an angry or hateful or hurting heart can last a lifetime, if we let it. When we pray we are challenged to leave those weapons behind for good and to believe—even in light of all the evidence to the contrary—in the power of love. Then one day there will be peace in our world, simply because all people will decide, finally, not to kill anyone anymore.

Interviewing the Dog III

When we were kids, most of us assumed that the patterns of behavior exhibited in our own homes were the same in every household. My dad, for example, would take a monster nap every Saturday right after he and my mom did the weekly grocery shopping. The thing was, Dad never napped in his own bed. He would choose a bedroom and a bed and crash for two hours or more. It would be unremarkable for any one of us to walk into his or her bedroom at four in the afternoon and see Dad stripped to his underwear sleeping in one of our beds. We just learned to work around him. I thought every father did this.

When it came to eating dinner though, my brothers and sisters and I knew our dining habits were, well, not normal. Sure, meals were prepared and served and consumed within a defined period of time, but that was about where the Hannons got off the train and took alternate transportation. My brothers and sisters and I—my mother and father are not to be blamed for this, God knows they tried—were pigs. But we were likeable pigs, thankful pigs, pigs without guile.

You would have thought our mother never fed us. I'll never forget one evening when Mom and Dad actually hosted a dinner party in *our* home. Dad had invited a number of his lawyer buddies and their wives over for steaks and baked potatoes.

We kids thought this was the most exotic thing we had ever seen. We tried to sneak peaks, but we'd get that patented glare from our mother that even from ten yards away commanded, "Back off and get into your room." The men were in suits and ties; the ladies wore dresses. My mom actually had makeup on. By the sound of it, it was a grand party. The muffled conversation, the bursts of laughter, the sound of our mother's and father's voices as they engaged in adult banter washed over us children like warm waves of water.

Before we could stop her, however, eleven-year-old Sally made her way to the dining room table, having judged that a sufficient amount of eating had occurred. She went up to one of my parents' dinner guests and, pointing to the half-eaten steak on his plate, inquired, "Can I have your bone?" I don't remember if the man surrendered the steak bone to my sister, but I am sure my parents were absolutely mortified.

WE WERE LIKEABLE PIGS, THANKFUL PIGS, PIGS WITHOUT GUILE.

But Sally didn't really know any better. Whenever we had steak, we were constantly hovering over each other's plates ready to pounce on neglected half-eaten carcasses. Dad himself inspected individual bones to make sure all the meat was consumed before we could ask for more. My parents should have been relieved that my sister hadn't also asked for the shelled-out potato skins. (Slap a healthy dollop of butter onto one of those babies, cram it in your mouth, and you have tasted a bit of heaven.)

It worked this way in our house: We said grace before any food was served, then

Mom would dole out the portions herself and serve her pack, oldest to youngest. By the time Mom got to me or one of my two younger sisters, the eldest, Brian and Sally, were already asking for seconds. This helps to explain why the older sibs were, well, big-boned.

We ate virtually all of our meals at the kitchen table, a long, sturdy, wood-slatted table with two long wooden benches on either side. Four of us sat on each side, and Julie reigned in the highchair on the far end. Mom would occasionally join us at the other end. Dad took his dinners in relative tranquility in the living room, using the time to watch the evening news and catch up on his reading. He made up for his dinner absences by joining us for weekday breakfasts and on the weekends when he was in a more relaxed mood.

There were only three occasions during the year when we assembled at the dining room table: Thanksgiving, Christmas and Easter. The girls wore dresses; the sport-coated boys wore ties. These three meals stood in stark contrast to the hundreds of meals we ate in the kitchen each year. One particular Christmas dinner stands out for all of us, back in 1970. We relive that meal every year—our own Hannon Passover so to speak—because, well, we have it on tape.

Earlier in the morning, thirteen-year-old Mike had unwrapped the present he hoped he was getting: an audio cassette recorder. He pretended he was Oakland Raider radio announcer Bill King, interviewing us all day as if we were Hall of Famers and offering real-time commentary while Mom was cooking the Christmas feast in the kitchen. ("Ladies and Gentlemen, we are here in the Hannon kitchen as Monica

Hannon is stuffing the turkey. Look at those hands! Monica, may we have a word?")
Mike also ran up and down the street getting neighbors to tell him what they really
thought of Richard M. Nixon.

What none of us knew as we sat down for dinner that late afternoon was that Mike
had hidden his recorder behind the flower arrangement on the buffet right near the
table, its "record" tab pushed down. Only when the pumpkin pies were brought out
did Mike inform us that the whole meal had been taped. We were absolutely delighted.

I'll wager we have listened to that Christmas tape dozens of times since then, and
it never ceases to amaze us how that one dinner revealed so much about who we
were as individuals and as a family.
Dad really was the quietest amongst
us all. We had to force him to join

NONE OF US CAN REFUTE
THIS. IT'S ALL ON TAPE.

with us in singing "Rudolph, the Red-Nosed Reindeer." Mom was the leader of the
band, Sally was bossy and too interested (as far as any of us were concerned) in the
food left on other people's plates, Greg was the clown, Jack and Mike were pugilis-
tic, Brian was authoritative, Mary was demure, Margaret and Julie were annoying,
and I was precociously irritating and (my siblings never let me forget) a bit of the
whiner. None of us can refute this. It's all on tape.

Later that evening, after we had listened to Mike's tape, the fun really began. We
put the tape recorder back on and did crazy things we had never done before: we
sang Christmas carols and asked funny questions of each other; we became comedic

actors trying to outdo each other; we pelt-
ed our parents with questions about the
early years when they first met, first dated,
first kissed ("What kind of kisser was she,
Dad?"). We wanted it all down on tape. We
knew this opportunity might never come

SIMPLY BY BEING FAITHFUL
TO THE BREAKING OF THE
BREAD, WE BUILD THE
KINGDOM AND RENEW
THE FACE OF THE EARTH.

our way again, so we took full advantage. We even interviewed our pooch, the ill-
tempered scrawny excuse for a Chihuahua named "Bambi." You see, if you held the
dog in your arms as Sally did when her turn came, stuck the microphone in its face,
asked a question like, "Tell us, Bambi, what do you think of Sally? Do you like Sally?"
and then pinch it really good on its butt, Bambi would growl and then let loose with
a bark. On tape it actually sounds like the dog is answering the questions—after
thoughtful pause—with canine sincerity. In Sally's case, however, the dog nearly bit
her nose off. We have it all on tape.

Over the years, listening to that Christmas dinner tape has assumed religious significance for us. First, it links us to our parents, both of whom have gone to God.
We get to hear their voices—unscripted, genuine and alive. But we also get to relive
those halcyon days in a way that makes the past very real and present. In addition,
my brothers' and sisters' kids get to hear what their parents sounded like when they
were just kids themselves. To see the looks on my nieces' and nephews' faces when
they hear our voices, you would think they were eavesdropping on the Last Supper.
It is humbling and a bit unnerving, but it is always a deeply joyful experience to let

the past become present—unvarnished and naked, free of interpretation or revision.

It is a good thing that audiocassettes were not around when Jesus was alive. Instead, all we have is the testimony of the four evangelists. In the absence of an audio cassette recorder, it is left to each of us to tell and retell the stories first told by our ancestors in faith, to memorize them with our hearts, to gather at the table often and break bread together (because Jesus wants us to), and with the Holy Spirit's help to renew the ancient covenant that unites our very lives with the life of our Father in heaven. Simply by being faithful to the breaking of the bread, we build the kingdom and renew the face of the earth.

Every time we gather at a table for a meal—and it doesn't matter if it is around the kitchen or dining room table, at the Waldorf Astoria, or in the café down the street—that meal draws us back to that Last Supper Jesus shared with his disciples before he died. For if one thing is true about our Christian faith it is this: Every meal is sacred.

CHAPTER SEVEN

Vespers
Sunset
Family

For as the heavens are high above the earth,

so great is his steadfast love toward those who fear him;

as far as the east is from the west,

so far he removes our transgressions from us.

As a father has compassion for his children,

so the LORD *has compassion for those who fear him.*

For he knows how we were made; he remembers that we are dust.

As for mortals, their days are like grass; they flourish like a flower of the field;

for the wind passes over it, and it is gone, and its place knows it no more.

But the steadfast love of the LORD

is from everlasting to everlasting on those who fear him,

and his righteousness to their children's children,

to those who keep his covenant and remember to do his commandments.

Psalm 103

I   *The Long Way Home*

When Eric Hamilton was seventeen years old, someone drove by one summer evening and shot him while he was sitting on the front stoop of his aunt's house. Though I read about it in the paper a couple of days later, the story of Eric Hamilton didn't come home to me until another week had passed and I got a phone call from a young woman named Yvonne, his girlfriend. As I was soon to find out, many people loved Eric Hamilton in his short life—just not the ones I had expected. We met, Yvonne and Eric's circle of friends and I, on a Friday around a table, and we broke bread and shared a cup and feasted on the friendship and family with whom God had seen fit to bless Eric. The feast of Eucharist has never been the same for me since, and I have Eric to thank for that.

You see, Eric lived mostly on the streets. On occasion a friend or relative would take him in for a couple of days, but for the most part Eric was content to live in an old Chevy he had bought for three hundred bucks from a gas station owner in Jackson, Mississippi, the day he turned sixteen. His stepdad had kicked him out of the house after a fight, and Eric, tired I suppose from all the beatings, figured he would go it alone. He moved to Oakland, California, where an anonymous alley shined in comparison to the hell his own home offered. In the six months Eric lived on the Oakland streets, he surrounded himself with a motley crew of ear-pierced punks and tie-dyed teenagers who traded personal horror stories like collectors trade baseball cards. On that Friday, we all gathered at the church to remember him.

They came in groups of four and five, puffing cigarettes and huddled together like lost sheep just outside the church. The boys fidgeted with the ties that hung around their necks like nooses; the girls adjusted their nylons. They looked older, almost dignified, in their demeanor, rightly judging the sobriety of the occasion. Eric's blood relatives from Oakland had decided not to hold any funeral service, leaving his adopted street kin to figure out on their own how they might do the work of grief—how

MANY PEOPLE LOVED ERIC HAMILTON IN HIS SHORT LIFE—JUST NOT THE ONES I HAD EXPECTED.

they might, as one of them told me, let Eric know that he counted, that he touched people while he was alive. So they came to church and asked if they might celebrate a memorial Mass for him. It was as if an ancient voice had beckoned them to the one place that promised, if not answers, at least hope. And so they came.

They came even though for most if not all of them it had been a very long time since they had been to church. Milling around outside as the church bells struck five in the evening, they seemed unsure of the next move. So I went outside and invited them to come in. Being good Catholics they spread out in twos and threes among a dozen different pews, keeping the first few rows empty. The gospel passage they had chosen came from the Gospel of John in which Jesus encourages his disciples not to let their hearts be troubled when he leaves them; Jesus reminded them that in God's house there were many rooms and that he would go and prepare a place for each of them. This passage was particularly poignant given the fact that the only room Eric could call his own when he died was the back seat of a beat up, rusted sedan.

We gathered for Eucharist, which means "thanksgiving." If you had been there you would have cried at the sight of thirty or so teenagers—with hands in pockets or holding on to handkerchiefs—slowly making the trek to the table, appearing as if it had taken them their whole lives to make it back home. I saw precious children of God: sad, angry, afraid, with wounds exposed and eyes that betrayed a longing for hope. They looked like what we all look like when our hearts are broken,

> I COULDN'T EXPLAIN IT EXCEPT THAT MAYBE I WAS SEEING THEM THE WAY GOD SEES THEM.

when our wounds mirror the wounds of Christ. This circle of brothers and sisters, drawn to the table by a deep hunger, took on the air of angels that Friday evening, and I couldn't explain it except that maybe I was seeing them the way God sees them. The kingdom of God began to make a little more sense to me as I witnessed this ragtag circle of delinquents holding hands and praying the Our Father together around a table in a place that was the closest thing to a home many of them had seen in quite awhile.

They came forward and tasted the Bread of Life, and as hungry as their souls were I would have let them come back for seconds if they had had the inclination. By the final blessing, the young men wept and mascara ran down the cheeks of the young women. They left the church that evening with great reluctance, holding and hugging each other, thankful that there was a place in the world that would make them feel so at home.

The Church has always taught that we are most authentically ourselves when we gather for Eucharist. It is wisdom born of a Spirit that sees through all the masks that hide us, all the walls that divide us, all the fear that leaves us thinking we have no home. Goodness and holiness are matters of the heart. If we wish to be the Body of Christ we must be about the work of cultivating hearts of love, hearts of mercy and forgiveness, hearts of acceptance and hospitality. We must be about the work of preparing rooms for those tired from the journey.

At around seven o'clock that Friday evening, almost an hour after the memorial Mass for Eric Hamilton had ended, all those young men and women were still there in front of the church—talking, laughing a little, smoking cigarettes. They didn't want to leave. It dawned on me that under our very noses the Holy Spirit was at work. Here was a scattering of teenagers, most baptized into the Catholic faith, none of whom would claim they had kept many of the rules of the Church very well. Looking at them, I couldn't help but think that somewhere inside they felt clean and pure and right with God, maybe for the first time in a long time. They felt at home because they knew they had not been condemned or made to feel outside the circle of God's warm embrace. That is a good thing. That is prayer in its purest form.

II California Highway 39

The longest road I ever traveled was that part of Highway 39 that connects Klamath Falls, Oregon, to Tulelake, California. It is a stretch of road that cuts through high desert, mountain lakes, and patchwork fields of potatoes and wheat and barley. It's around thirty miles from the Greyhound bus station in Klamath Falls to our family's ancestral farmhouse, just a stone's throw from downtown Tulelake. But on that March evening of 1980, the road might has well have been thousands and thousands of miles long. It seemed to take forever to get to the farm that night.

I arrived for spring break, a swaggering, swashbuckling sophomore home from the University of Portland, filled with great ideas and grand plans, a kid who seemed to fit only too well the title *sophomore,* which is roughly translated from the Greek "a wise moron." Mom and Dad, dressed in blue jeans and work boots and heavy plaid wool shirts, met me at the bus station. They looked like something out of the T.V. show *Green Acres.*

The previous summer Dad had retired after more than twenty-five years as a lawyer. He hung up his tie the day he retired and never wore one again. Soon after, they sold the house in Castro Valley, our hometown, and moved north to the farmhouse in which my dad had grown up. It had fallen into disrepair, having lain vacant for the better part of fifteen years. But you could tell by looking at my parents dressed the way they were—traces of dirt under their fingernails, smiles that rested so easily upon their faces—that they were content in their relative poverty. Thoreau's admonition to a hectic, overworked society to "simplify, simplify" found a receptive home in my parents' hearts. A big day for them now was chopping down trees for firewood or setting traps for mice and rats and other vermin.

The drive home started out well. Mom told me about the trip to Reno, Nevada, that she and Dad had taken the previous month and how she had won two hundred bucks on the slot machines. Dad described his daily routine of walking into town twice a day to get the mail and stopping at the Sportsman Bar and Grill for steak and beer with his old grade school pals who had never left the little town. I felt very close to my parents that evening—sitting in the back seat of their mud-caked '78 Cutlass, listening to them go on about their new life, and watching the sun set behind purple hills. It was all so peaceful. Then, as they say, all hell broke loose.

> BUT ON THAT MARCH EVENING OF 1980, THE ROAD MIGHT HAS WELL HAVE BEEN THOUSANDS AND THOUSANDS OF MILES LONG. IT SEEMED TO TAKE FOREVER TO GET TO THE FARM THAT NIGHT.

It was seven o'clock; so Dad switched the radio on to listen to the news on the hour. Leading off was the ongoing saga of the fifty-three American hostages held in

Iran, and after that came a report on the occupation of Afghanistan by Soviet troops. I told my parents about the huge rally the previous week at my university during which hundreds of students protested President Carter's reinstatement of the draft, and I criticized President Carter's decision to keep the United States out of the 1980 Olympics that summer. I could see Mom's knuckles turn white as her grip on the steering wheel grew tighter as I spoke. I'm sure she was wondering how far out I was willing to swim in the shark-infested waters of political discussion with my Republican father.

Have you ever been in an argument when just as you're saying something you know immediately that it was the wrong thing to say—but you can't stuff the words back into your mouth? That's what happened to me. I remember saying, in a rather nonchalant sort of way, "Well, Dad, you know, I'm a pacifist. It's against my beliefs to participate in war. I would be a conscientious objector if I were ever drafted." Thud. Dad turned the radio off and sat there in complete silence. Uh, oh. I began to fill the silence with everything I had learned about Emerson and Thoreau and Gandhi. I expounded on our Church's long tradition of nonviolent resistance and pacifism. I even threw in a bunch of saints and Jesus himself, but my dad would hear none of it. His face was turning red and his words came out cutting: "You're telling me you would run away, that you would be a coward?" Well, that didn't sit well with me, being my father's son, so I turned it up a notch by calling into question my dad's own commitment to Jesus' message of love and reconciliation and forgiveness. In the end I knew there would be only carnage. I had tapped into some deep vein of patriotism in my father, forgetting that my sophisticated lawyer, city-dwelling dad was first a farm boy schooled in rural, corn-fed values and unquestioning loyalty to flag and country. As my mother was putting the pedal to the metal, hoping to reach home before our argument deteriorated into blows, Dad turned around and faced me. He said, "I'll tell you this: If you were ever to resist the draft, you would no longer be a son of mine." My response was equally harsh. "Fine," I said as I leaned forward, our noses almost touching. "Who needs a father who would so easily disown his own son!" Then I slumped back in my seat, utterly destroyed.

The last five miles were spent in complete silence. I looked out onto the night with tears in my eyes and a knife in my heart. And though I couldn't see my father, I'm sure he was equally devastated. Don't think the irony escaped me, even then, that in my attempt to speak passionately about peace and nonviolence, love and reconciliation, I had entered a battle with my father that left us both deeply wounded.

> ON THE EVENING OF THE THIRD DAY, DAD ANNOUNCED THAT HE AND I WERE GOING TO DIG A WELL THAT NEXT MORNING. I JUST SHRUGGED MY SHOULDERS.

We didn't speak for three days, my dad and I. How do you bridge the deep canyon of hurt that sometimes divides father and son, mother and daughter, parent and child? Meals were eaten in silence or not at all. Dad spent time at the Sportsman Bar and Grill while I sat at home, bending my mother's ear and resisting her pleading to at least meet Dad halfway. On the evening of the third day, however, Dad announced that he and I were going to dig a well that next morning. I just shrugged my shoulders.

We started digging at dawn. First I dug a hole three feet long, three feet wide and three feet deep, laughing with morbid humor at the thought that Dad had cleverly gotten me to dig my own grave. When it passed my father's inspection, we began, with the help of our post-hole digger, to dig the actual well. It really is a two-man operation, because after a while you attach more and more poles to the post-hole digger, allowing it to reach

> DAD AND I WERE LIKE LITTLE KIDS, PATTING EACH OTHER ON THE SHOULDER AND BETRAYING SHEEPISH GRINS, NOT WANTING TO BE TOO PROUD OF OUR STUNNING ACHIEVEMENT.

deeper into the earth, tapping the deep reservoir of water in the ground. You create such suction digging so deeply that it requires four strong arms to pull the poles out.

By sundown, my father and I had built our forty-foot-deep well. We had taken three different trips to the hardware store to purchase cement, the well piping, and the pump. We had followed all the directions meticulously, and by seven o'clock that evening, Mom's beautiful front lawn and flowerbeds were being soaked by our well water. That night we had steaks for dinner, and the conversation turned to wells and water tables and how easy it was to build a well when you think about it. Politics never came up.

Dad must have caught the home improvement bug that week, because a couple of days later he decided that we needed a few more outlets in the house—and by God we didn't need some electrician to come in and do what we could easily do on our own, what with our brains and common sense. We spent the whole day putting in the wiring, having purchased the 150 feet of 220 wiring at the hardware store in town. I spent the afternoon on my back under the house feeding wiring to my dad, who was barking instructions at me from inside the house. We ended up putting in a new outlet in the kitchen, one in the bedroom, and a third in the living room. Dad and I were so excited. We had saved hundreds and hundreds of dollars doing this ourselves.

At the appointed time, Mom plugged the toaster into the new outlet in the kitchen and the vacuum into the new outlet in the living room. With a flip of the switch, the vacuum roared to life, the dim light on the front of the vacuum shining in sweet victory. Dad and I were like little kids, patting each other on the shoulder and betraying sheepish grins, not wanting to be too proud of our stunning achievement.

The toaster exploded right about the time the light on the vacuum grew brighter and brighter. Mom quickly unplugged the vacuum and retrieved the fire extinguisher to put out the little fire on the kitchen counter. The electrician told us the next day that the house was wired for 110 volts and that basically Dad and I were pumping in enough electricity to light Wrigley Field. Of course, we were completely crestfallen and defeated, mere shells of our former selves; it took every ounce of energy for my dad to write out the check to the electrician. We spent the rest of the afternoon at the Sportsman, buying each other beers in a dark corner, keeping the story to ourselves.

Late in the afternoon that Saturday, I left to go back to school. Dad drove me to the Greyhound station by himself, having spent thirty minutes in the kitchen making me three or four roast beef sandwiches for the long trip. We had a good laugh on the way, recounting how we almost burned the farmhouse down earlier in the week. We enjoyed each other's company as we

I THANKED GOD THE FATHER THAT HE HAD SEEN FIT TO BRING MY FATHER AND ME TOGETHER AGAIN.

drove that thirty miles, talking about wells and wiring, life on the farm, and schoolwork. We arrived at the bus depot just as the sun was descending over the hills. We stood in front of each other looking at our shoes, our hands dug deeply into our pockets. I finally looked up to my dad and said, "Well, I better be heading out." And my dad said, "Yep, I guess it's time to go." I reached out to shake his hand, but Dad, with calm and grace, reached out with his arms. He hugged me tight and kissed me on the cheek. I don't ever remember my father doing that before, at least since I could walk. I told my dad I loved him, and he told me he loved me too; and with the biggest lump I ever had in my throat I climbed into the bus and waved goodbye. Dad was dressed in his worn jeans, plaid shirt, and John Deere cap and was standing next to his still-caked-in-mud Cutlass. I thanked God the Father that He had seen fit to bring my father and me together again.

The bridge that brought me back to my father and he back to me was constructed of very simple materials—around 150 feet of electrical wiring, forty feet of plas-
tic pipe, a few roast beef sandwiches, and a kiss on the cheek. These human con-
structions are essentially prayer. They speak to God of pain and shame and hurt, and
of hope and healing and peace and forgiveness. That kiss was one of the most pow-
erful prayers my father ever prayed. Being held by my father and feeling that kiss, I wasn't sure if there was anything sweet-

> THAT'S THE WAY IT IS WITH GOD—
> STOPPING AT NOTHING TO HEAL
> WHATEVER WOUND WE MAY BE
> NURSING, SECRETLY OR OTHERWISE.

er in life. It was homecoming for both of us. I who bore my father's name was his son
after all and would always be. And he would always be my father. That's the way it
is with God—stopping at nothing to heal whatever wound we may be nursing,
secretly or otherwise. The road back to God, much like California Highway 39 that
my father and I traveled together, is always paved with mercy. Despite how long the
road seems at times, in the end it always brings us home.

III Family Values

Over twenty years ago, I made the choice to become part of a nontraditional family: the Congregation of Holy Cross. Our founder, Venerable Basil Moreau, was a man way ahead of his time. In the mid-1800s, he brought together a group of diocesan priests from the French countryside and joined them with the fledgling Brothers of Saint Joseph to form his new Congregation. He also founded the Sisters of Holy Cross and was intent on having all three branches united under one banner and one rule. From the beginning he saw the priests, brothers and sisters of Holy Cross as a family. This was an unprecedented move, for men's and women's communities were, canonically speaking, segregated. While Basil Moreau's dream was never realized canonically, we in Holy Cross still speak of each other in familial terms. Basil would be proud. I am first a Hannon, but I am also a Holy Cross religious and priest, a member of a worldwide family.

I freely chose to embrace the religious vows of poverty, chastity and obedience in the Congregation of Holy Cross because I had come to know, love and admire the men and women of the order. For me, the litmus test was a simple one: Are these people happy?

In my younger days, I was an idealistic fool. My brother Brian told me once that when he first arrived at college he honestly hoped he would come to know all things. At twenty-two I was equally ambitious, except that what I wanted was to change the world. I had long felt a stirring in my heart, which I interpreted as God's voice suggesting that I at least look at the priesthood. I had been educated by Holy Cross brothers in high school and Holy Cross priests in college, so I naturally turned to Holy Cross first. These were men with fire in their hearts and in their bellies. If I was going to change the world, Holy Cross was the religious community for me.

I remember the first time I told Dad I was going to apply for entrance into the seminary at Notre Dame. My parents were visiting me in Portland, Oregon, in my senior year at the University of Portland. Dad and I were sitting in the bar at the Benson Hotel downtown. I took hold of my glass of beer and raised it up. "A toast," I said to him, and he raised his glass of bourbon and water.

"What's the toast?" my father asked.

"I'm going to study for the priesthood," I said, and we clinked our glasses. As I took a long, nervous gulp of beer—wondering how my father the lawyer was going react—he said with a wry grin on his face, "You know there's not a lot of money in that line of work," and we both laughed. Then he got serious and asked me, "Are you going to be happy?" I said that I would, and that was that. (Of course, I already knew that my mom would be thrilled because it is the hope of every Irish-Catholic mother that one of her sons be a priest, but I could tell her concern mirrored my dad's. All parents hope that their children will be happy in their lives and their life's work.)

There is a saying in Holy Cross that I think applies to any life commitment, whether it is priesthood, religious life, or marriage: The reasons you come are almost always different from the reasons you stay. I came to Holy Cross because I wanted to change the world. It wasn't too long before I figured out that it was going to take longer than I initially anticipated. The world, like almost all of us who inhabit it, doesn't take kindly to change. So while there will always be a burning passion in my heart for building the kingdom of God on this earth, I stayed in Holy Cross and now expect to eventually take my place in the community cemetery at the University of Notre Dame for a very simple reason: The men of Holy Cross bring out the very best in me.

My brothers in Holy Cross are men of immense talent and creativity. They work their tails off because they love to work. They write books and teach and run parishes and schools and minister to the sick and dying and to the poorest of the poor. They work in prisons and jails and retreat centers. But honestly, what I love most about them is the laughter. When Fr. John Gerber, the rector of the seminary, told us on our first day that in joining Holy Cross we were joining a family, one that would mirror in many ways the kinds of families from which we came, I was at first a little concerned. If the Hannon family was going to be the role model for my new family, then I still would be having my share of arguments and fights. It meant things in Holy Cross were going to be loud and boisterous; it meant we were going to get on each other's nerves every now and then; it meant there would be many opportunities for forgiveness; but it also meant we were going to laugh a lot.

This has all been borne out. Fr. Gerber was right. I love being a Holy Cross priest because I get to live and work with men who are pretty darn comfortable in their own skins, who dare me to reach beyond my grasp, who inspire me by their generous spirit and their desire to serve. In the Constitution on Brotherhood in the Rule of Holy Cross is an admonition that I have come to cherish: "It is essential to our mission that we strive to abide so attentively together that people will observe: 'See how they love another.' We will then be a sign in an alienated world: men who have, for love of their LORD, become closest neighbors, trustworthy friends, brothers."

> ALL PARENTS HOPE THAT THEIR CHILDREN WILL BE HAPPY IN THEIR LIVES AND THEIR LIFE'S WORK.

These days I live and work at Notre Dame High School with Fr. Bill Brinker, eighty-four years young, who in his forty-eighth year at the school continues to counsel students and tutor them. I live with Fr. Jerry Esper—our keeper of The Story—who can, at the drop of a hat, tell you any story about any Holy Cross priest or brother of the past forty-five years. I live with Fr. Rich Conyers, an art and architecture historian for whom no pun is too irritating to leave unspoken. I live with Brother Pat Lynch, an Irish expatriate who is quick with the slightly off-colored joke or song and thinks nothing of picking you up at O'Hare at three in the morning. I live with Fr. Chris Kuhn, twenty-seven years a teacher of freshmen, who is my kindred spirit in politics. (We're both Roosevelt Democrats.) I live with Fr. Mike DeLaney, who can speak five languages fluently and whose sole purpose in life seems to be to make everyone feel at home. I live with Fr. David Scheidler, half German and half Mexican, who makes friends and keeps them because he has a loyal heart. I live with Brother Paul Benarczyk, who is wise beyond his years and gracious and generous and makes a chili that will grow hair on your chest. I live with Fr. Leonard Rozario, a native of Bangladesh, who is getting a degree in linguistics and is for me a window to another culture. Fr. Don McNeill is a part of our community, though he lives and works now most of the time in the Pilsen neighborhood on the near West Side of Chicago. He is a giant of a man in Holy Cross, a priest of immense talent who astounds me by his humility. And then I live with Phil Donner, a Holy Cross seminarian who is spending two years with us teaching at the high school. (He is only twenty-five years old, so he doesn't really know yet what he's gotten himself into.)

I live and work with these men. We are brothers to each other. We fight with each other and forgive each other. We share a common table and a common purse. We pray with and for each other, and we try our best to give each other the support we need to face the world each day with hope. But most of all we are men who can lay our burdens down long enough to share a moment of laughter and joy. In all of this, we are in many respects like every other family: At our best we bring out the best in each other, and bringing out the best in each other is just another form of prayer.

CHAPTER EIGHT

Compline
Nine in the Evening
Completion

Happy are those who do not follow the advice of the wicked,

or take the path that sinners tread, or sit in the seat of scoffers;

but their delight is in the law of the LORD,

and on his law they meditate day and night.

They are like trees planted by streams of water,

which yield their fruit in its season, and their leaves do not wither.

In all that they do, they prosper.

Psalm 1

Whittling the Legs Down

It seemed very strange to be kneeling in front of a casket. I had never done this before, but here he was lying in front of me in religious and sacerdotal state, and there I was doing what I supposed was expected of one aspiring to religious life and priesthood. Except for the cadaver I once got to see in college when some nursing student friends of mine snuck me in, I had never spied a dead body before, save those I saw in newspapers or magazines or on television. I was twenty-three and felt very lucky that no one close to me had been touched by death.

Fr. Greg Stegmeyer, CSC, was a rather controversial figure, from what I could gather from those who knew him in Holy Cross. Actually, the truth was that you either loved him or hated him. He was either a dictator, intolerant of any debate or discussion, or a prophet, refreshingly bold and courageous and countercultural, with fingers pressed firmly against the pulse of the gospel. As the Superior to seminarians preparing for a life of mission in Bengal, he assigned rooms with didactic flair. For example, the newest seminarians were assigned the largest, most spacious rooms; those who had survived the grueling training—the third-year theologians and the deacons—were given the smallest. Fr. Greg believed the older you got the less stuff you needed and the more unencumbered you should be. It was a lesson I am sure most of these Holy Cross missionaries took with them as they got off the train in Delhi or Dandora with a suitcase in one hand and a breviary in the other.

So here was Fr. Greg, resting in the coffin before me. I knew what lay before me was an empty shell, but I was hoping that a bit of his spirit was still hanging around—maybe only a mere hint of his life's breath—for I was young and wanted to learn from that spirit. I was spending a few minutes praying for a man I barely knew, whose entire life had been distilled down to one story told earlier that evening at his wake by a fellow Holy Cross priest who was his friend. My hunch—my hope—based solely on this one story was that Fr. Greg would have been my friend too.

He was young back then: tall, handsome, filled with fire. The founder of the Congregation of Holy Cross, Venerable Basil Moreau, defined zeal as "that flame of burning desire to make God known, loved and served." By that measure, Fr. Greg was a zealot his whole life. By the time he retired from active ministry, he had spent half a century in Bengal. He toiled in the vineyards of India, Pakistan and Bangladesh. Even when gravity started working on him and he grew more brittle, the flame of holy desire never flickered in him.

This man, who as a young seminarian would lead like-hearted comrades into the Cumberland hills of Maryland on summer afternoon breaks to hunt rattlesnakes, became the priest who later in life would be asked to leave several dioceses in Bengal because the bishops grew tired of his indefatigable zeal as a Vatican II reformer. Fr. Greg was a stirrer of pots, a disrupter of apple carts, and he was that way from the very beginning.

So here is the story I first heard the day he was waked:

When Fr. Greg Stegmeyer first stepped into the small, remote Indian village chapel upon his arrival as pastor, the first thing he noticed was that except for the altar, presider's chair, and the table on which the tabernacle rested, the rest of the church was devoid of furniture. That is, except for two sturdy benches leaning against the back wall of the church. That Sunday, as the village Catholics gathered for Mass, he was quick to notice that those benches were reserved for the wealthiest of the village, those who carried themselves with an air of superiority born of high social status. This didn't sit well with Fr. Greg. So the following weekend before Mass, he went into the church when no one was looking and got rid of the two benches in the back and his presider's chair as well.

Folks walking into the church that Sunday morning immediately became disoriented. At first they thought they had been burglarized, but when young Pastor Greg informed them it was his doing, a riot practically ensued.

TO TOLERATE THE PRESENCE OF THOSE BENCHES IN A HOUSE OF CHRISTIAN WORSHIP WAS A SIN, AND NOT A SMALL ONE AT THAT.

The village elite refused to sit on the ground with the rest of the faithful; the village poor jumped up and down like they were walking barefoot on hot coals. Eyes darted back and forth, and in the gathering heat and combustion old ladies fainted. Fr. Greg, though, stood his ground.

That evening and for several more nights, the village chief and the elders pleaded with Fr. Greg to bring the benches back. The social fabric of the whole village had been torn asunder. The very foundation of order that had supported the peaceful life of the village as far back as anyone could remember was crumbling before their very eyes. Fr. Greg began to wonder if he had overreached. Long before the world was graced with "What would Jesus Do?" bracelets, Fr. Greg prayed long into that last night before Sunday. He asked the LORD to give him direction, to guide his young heart. Guide the LORD did. That Sunday morning, nervous village parishioners arrived at the church to find the benches back in their old place. Delighted, they sang full-throated and deep and long at Mass. Rich and poor alike mingled outside afterwards for an hour, relieved and, in an odd sort of way, invigorated—like survivors of a plane crash or an earthquake. Everyone was happy that the crisis was over and not a little relieved that they were alive to tell about it.

Fr. Greg, however, was not happy. As far as he was concerned, it was not over. Those benches remained a scandal to the Christian gospel. In Christ, he would say, there is no Greek or Jew, slave or free, rich or poor. All are one in Christ. To tolerate the presence of those benches in a house of Christian worship was a sin, and not a small one at that. So that night Fr. Greg made the solitary stroll from his house to the church. There he sat on the ground before the Blessed Sacrament and prayed for the flock he pastored. He prayed that he might be a good shepherd of souls. He prayed that his congregation might someday erase the lines that divided them, that one day they might have the courage to remove those damned benches themselves. And then, as he left, he took a small metal file from his cassock and gently filed the thinnest layer of wood from the bottom of the legs of those benches.

He did this for ten years. Every night, Fr. Greg would shave off the merest sliver of wood from the bottom of those benches, a layer imperceptible to the naked eye. Every week, the community would gather for Mass and the elders would sit on those benches and the rest would sit on the ground. What they didn't know—what no one knew except God and Fr. Greg—was that those benches were marching inexorably toward the ground at the rate of maybe an inch a year. Finally, one day in Ordinary Time, Fr. Greg's prayers were answered. Without fuss or fanfare, the chief and elders of the village had the benches removed. They served no practical purpose, since they were so close to the ground.

Over fifty years later, as I knelt at his casket in the seminary chapel, I imagined seeing Fr. Greg as that young Holy Cross priest, sitting in a chair outside the door of his house in that Indian village, smoking a cigar, the collar of his habit unbuttoned and loose. I imagined his was a countenance of sanguine contentment, for his flock, the people he had grown to love and cherish, were one. It was not his victory but the Lord's, and whatever glory there might be in that victory, in seeing those benches chopped up and made into something useful like firewood, that glory was the Lord's as well. Fr. Greg had seen it through to the end, this devious, holy little plan to change hearts one imperceptible fraction of an inch at a time. I couldn't help but think that he wouldn't have minded one bit if the Lord had called him home that very night.

A job well done, a life well lived and brought to completion. This, too, is prayer. It is a grand and glorious and silent prayer, like whittling wood in secret.

One Pitcher, One Batter, One Second in Kane County

I have long believed that Notre Dame High School for Boys in Niles, Illinois, is built on top of an ancient Illini sacred burial ground. There is no other way to explain the mind-numbing, heart-wrenching defeats over the past fifty years at the hands of our bitter rivals. Sure, the Dons of Notre Dame have had their share of athletic success, but up until June 12, 2004, it had never secured a single Illinois High School Association (IHSA) state championship in any sport.

For an all-boys high school, sports are a religion. Add to the mix the fact that the school is run by the Priests of the Congregation of Holy Cross, the same religious order that founded the University of Notre Dame, and you have built-in from the very beginning a highly exalted sense of athletic manifest destiny.

For example, if you're an Irish fan you will never forget the day back in 1980 when Harry Oliver kicked a fifty-one-yard field goal (only the second field goal of his career) into the wind to beat Michigan with no time left on the clock. Fans at Notre Dame Stadium that brisk autumn day will swear on their mothers' graves that the wind mysteriously died down the very moment Oliver's cleats made contact with the pigskin. Is it any surprise (with "Touchdown Jesus" presiding over every home football game and rosary beads tangled in the fingers of sober priests and intoxicated freshmen) that most people believe (either begrudgingly or religiously) that Notre Dame enjoys an unfair advantage in the divine support department?

Folks are often reminded—as former ND football Coach Lou Holtz put it—that it doesn't matter to Jesus who wins or loses a football game. Jesus, after all, doesn't have favorites. Now, his mother, Holtz would remind his players, is a different story: Whether Notre Dame wins or not *does* matter to her!

So the Dons of Notre Dame (the Gentlemen of Our Lady) are a competitive tribe. They are tough and resilient and not easily intimidated. They hate to lose, but they understand that battles—whether on the field of competition or in the human heart—are sometimes won and sometimes lost. But for fifty years, losing "the big one" has been their story. Over ten thousand students have graduated from Notre Dame High School, and I'm willing to bet that more than five or six thousand of them were members of one athletic team or another. Yet not one of them held aloft in his trembling, triumphant arms an IHSA state championship trophy. Not one.

On June 12, 2004, one of them did.

Notre Dame's baseball team scratched and scraped and fought their way into the championship game that June evening against a tough and proven Joliet Catholic squad. To get to that final match, the Dons earlier that day had to erase a seven-run deficit against powerhouse Carmel High School to win the semifinal game 11-10. It was the greatest come-from-behind victory in state playoff history, with clutch hitting, amazing relief pitching, flawless defense. If you were there that morning, you had a feeling in your gut that the Dons had a rendezvous with history.

I didn't know what to do during the five-hour break between the semifinal and championship games. I was left to drive around Kane County in the far western suburbs of Chicago, alone with my thoughts. Tantalizing hopes danced in my head. Could this actually be happening? I knew every one of these players. Some of them I had taught. I had taken measure of their minds, of their hearts, of their backbones, but this was to be a lesson in the anatomy of hope. These boys possessed what can only be described as holy determination: teenaged boys prone to prank—yes; adolescent males saddled with daunting insecurities and fears—sure; young sojourners making their way in the world with unwrapped maps stuffed in their back pockets

SO THE DONS OF NOTRE DAME (THE GENTLEMEN OF OUR LADY) ARE A COMPETITIVE TRIBE. THEY ARE TOUGH AND RESILIENT AND NOT EASILY INTIMIDATED.

and compasses held gingerly in their sweaty palms—you bet. But they were something more. You saw it in their calm eyes and in their pursed lips. You saw it in the way they adjusted their baseball caps and kicked the dirt from their cleats and punched their mitts. You heard it in the confident tone of their voices as they spoke words of encouragement to their teammates. These were young men who believed in themselves.

A better way to put it, the way I would always remind them when we prayed together, is that their job was to give greater glory and honor to God. It wasn't about them. It was about what God could accomplish *through* them on the ball field or any other venue of their lives. This is, after all, the beauty of sports from a sacramental viewpoint: Sports offer yet another moment when elements of nature (human and otherwise) become a conduit for divine grace and we celebrate the awesome, ineffable, tangible presence of God in our midst. Sure there was a lot of praying going on in the stands and on the field that day, prayers of praise and prayers of desperation. But the most profound prayer that night was never spoken; it was uttered in action.

Senior Greg Reda hadn't thrown a pitch the entire playoffs. Not against Taft, Saint Patrick, Loyola, Evanston Township, Oak Park, Normal Community, or Carmel. But in this championship game, Coach Bob Kostuch pointed to the dugout and out Reda sprang to relieve the starting pitcher, who was obviously exhausted. It was the top of the third with two outs. The Dons had squandered a 3-0 lead and now were tied with the Hilltoppers 4-4. Reda took the next batter to a full count before striking him out to end the inning and stop the bleeding.

> BUT THE MOST PROFOUND PRAYER THAT NIGHT WAS NEVER SPOKEN; IT WAS UTTERED IN ACTION.

By the top of the seventh inning (the last one of the game), Reda had been masterful, retiring every batter he had faced save two: a hit batsman in the sixth and a leadoff walk in the seventh. With no one out and a man on first, Reda forced the next batter into a fielder's choice. He then struck out the next batter for the second out.

Meanwhile, the runner had managed to steal a couple of bases, so it was 6-4, a man on third, the tying run at the plate.

Ball one.

Ball two.

Ball three.

My heart was in my throat. *For the love of God, let's go, Greg!*

Swing, and a foul ball.

Swing, and another foul ball. Kane County Stadium was rocking by this time. Two thousand fans were on their feet, stomping and cheering. Players were jumping up and down in their respective dugouts. Still photographs would later document the final pitch. It came down to this: one pitcher, one batter, and one second in Kane County, Illinois.

I'll never forget that last second, right before Reda got the sign. I remember the sweat dripping off his face. I remember the ball slowly rotating in his pitching hand resting on his back while he leaned toward the plate, waiting. I remember he didn't—not for a millisecond—take his eyes off his catcher.

He began his motion and delivered. It was Reda's patented fastball on the outside corner of the plate. It had been his best friend all game. The umpire dutifully rung up the batter, and the celebration began.

There are in a life specific moments in time that are forever etched into our memory: the birth of a firstborn, the moment you say to another for the first time "I love you," a sunset or sip of wine or piece of music that leaves you joyfully stunned and speechless. These are moments when grace pierces gravity and reminds us that, as the poet Patrick Kavanaugh put it, "God is in the bits and pieces of Everyday." Thus we remember as well those moments laced with threads of sadness and pain: the loss of a friendship; the death of a loved one; a secret, monumental failure; the betrayals of youth; a missed opportunity. Even these moments carry with them hidden graces.

That one second before Greg Reda flung that last pitch to the plate was one of those moments for me—a moment of outlandish, preposterous, ridiculous grace, for that one second seemed to pierce the very veil of eternity. Wrapped into that one second was every hope and dream of every baseball player who ever played the game, indeed, every hope and dream of every person who ever dared to imagine something or someone greater than himself or herself. It was the last second of the last inning of the last game of a championship season, and in that moment's pause it seemed to me that everyone who ever lived paused in eternity's embrace and watched.

Even as I write this, I wonder if I have overreached, if my words, drenched in the syrup of hyperbole, ring true. And then I recall the details of that last second. Honestly, the power of that moment is still overwhelming. It was then, and is still now, a glorious prayer that marked the end of a long and arduous journey, and even better, it signaled the beginning of something new as well.

The Last Word

A few miles outside the small farming town of Tulelake, California, where my dad grew up, on a small mountain overlooking the vast valley below, stands a cross. You really have to want to see it to get to it because any path that might have been there is long gone. But there the cross stands, sixty years after it was planted into the earth. It was constructed out of what appears to be heavy railroad crossties and pieces of plywood and heavy wire to keep it all together. I remember my great-aunt, Aunty Ber, made reference to it when I was a young boy. She used to say that whenever my dad, her nephew, went missing on warmer days for any length of time as a child, he could usually be found at that cross. Apparently, it was a place he liked to go to read a book in peace, and later, when he was a teenager, a romantic venue where he could take a girl and kiss her without interruption or teasing from his brothers.

Years after listening to these old yarns from an old lady, I visited that cross. It was quite a hike from the road, and I arrived at the foot of the cross just as the sun was setting. A deep reddish orange with hints of pink and purple streaked the sky, and down below in the valley you could see the ripe wheat and barley swaying gently in the breeze and the dim headlights of pickups and tractors lumbering down the highway. I sat down and rested my body against the cross. I finally understood why my father came there as often as he did. From that odd perch, one that was marked by a cross, you could see, if you looked closely enough, a hint of Paradise.

Of course, to understand and appreciate this particular reminiscence fully, I should tell you that the cross of which I speak was constructed by Japanese prisoners who were detained at the Japanese Relocation Center in Tulelake from early 1942 until the spring of 1946. No one knows the names of the men who built it, but they had arrived in Tulelake, along with 18,000 other American citizens of Japanese descent living on the west coast, by virtue of an executive order issued by President Roosevelt. More a reaction of fear and wartime hysteria than ethnic hatred or intolerance, this order nonetheless stripped Japanese citizens—many born in the United States—of their jobs, their homes, their possessions, and their freedom. The relocation camp in Tulelake was only one of more than thirty in the western states.

I remember my mother recalling in vivid detail the day her next-door neighbors had to leave their home on Summit Street in Oakland. The parents had packed up the sedan, having taken everything they could possibly carry with them, and then with their four children—one of whom was my mother's age—drove to the train station, where they were to board a train that would take them to a camp in Utah. My mom, thirteen at the time, never saw them again.

Sitting at that cross, I saw those men trudging up the hill with heavy beams digging into their shoulders. I wondered if they too had fallen three times on the way up their Calvary. I tried to imagine what they were feeling in their hearts as they dug the hole into which they would set the cross and the tenor of their conversation as they raised the cross and secured it. Were they feelings and words of doubt and desperation, of anger and disillusionment, of resignation and regret? I do not believe they were any of those things. For my hunch is that these men, Christians all, harbored thoughts of mercy and forgiveness. Such things have the cross of Christ come to signify for those of us who believe.

In reflecting on the power of this cross, the one planted on the hill outside the gates of Jerusalem, I am reminded of the words Gandhi once uttered when faced with the overwhelming and intimidating power of the British. He said, "They may break my bones; they may torture my body; they may even kill me. Then they will have my dead body. But they will not have my obedience!" In the gospels we have clear and incontrovertible

WHEN ALL SEEMS LOST—WE ARE NEVER FORGOTTEN.

evidence that the Romans secured neither the humble surrender of Jesus nor his obedience. Instead of doing what he was supposed to do, which was to die a miserable and shameful death, Jesus chose to forgive. The evidence shows that Jesus absolved all those responsible for his untimely death: "Father, forgive them for they know not what they do." In Luke's gospel, Jesus even has a brief yet telling conversation with one of the hanging thieves that speaks of mercy and forgiveness. The thief calls Jesus by name, a sweet and touching detail, and in doing so reaches across a lifetime of sin and shame to cling in this last hour to the one person who might grab him and hold him lest he plunge into the abyss of darkness. "Jesus," the Good Thief begs, "remember me when you come into your kingdom."

I want you to imagine you are there at that cross. Close your eyes and picture this man—tears no doubt running down his cheeks, waiting in hope for Jesus to reply. See Jesus turn toward a human being who has spent most of his life running from God and assure him that he need run no more. For God has—even at this late hour—found him. "This very day, we shall walk together in the Garden of Paradise," Jesus promises. From his odd perch on the cross, Jesus gains Paradise and immediately shares it with another.

> IN THE END, JESUS' LAST WORD WOULD BE MERCY AND FORGIVENESS.

In the end, Jesus' last word would be mercy and forgiveness. The Roman rulers and Jewish leaders may have sneered at him; the soldiers and crowd at his feet may have jeered him; but he absorbed all that hatred and fear and reflected mercy instead, using the sign of the cross to show that in the end the power of love is always greater than the love of power. They could break his bones, torture him, even kill him. Then they would have his dead body. But they would not have his obedience.

And that is why I dare to believe that more than sixty years ago a handful of Japanese men, unjustly treated, dressed in humiliation and shame, could plant a cross on a hill and pray a prayer of hope and mercy, not despair and vengeance. The cross of Christ has a power all its own to soften the hardest of hearts, to silence the weapons of war, to be a powerful sign to a weary world that even in the midst of suffering and pain—when all seems lost—we are never forgotten. "This very day," Jesus reminds us as well, "you will be with me in Paradise."

Epilogue

One day I asked my four-teen-year-old freshmen students at Notre Dame High School for Boys, "Gentlemen, what is prayer?" We were focusing on the power of metaphor as a literary device, so I wanted them to tell me what prayer is, metaphorically speak-ing. Here is what they said.

Prayer is…

Climbing a mountain
The ending of *The Planet of the Apes*
A path to heaven
The Chicago Bull's "six-peat"
Painting a picture
Living under water without oxygen
Following your dreams
Coloring
A private chat room with God
Playing chess
Tug-of-War
A labyrinth
Waiting for Christmas
Aiming a flashlight in the dark
An escape route
Trying to get straight A's in school
Scoring a touchdown in football
A secret garden
A lifeline to God
A word puzzle
Surgery
A mirror
Building a fire

Prayer is a powerful, mysterious thing; it connects and reconnects the human with the divine and the divine with the human. It transcends time and space. Words to explain it or describe it must always in the end fail, for in the end words always get in the way. And so—quietly, silently, hopefully—we cling to the faithful notion that God is there somewhere, listening to us and speaking to us. And so pray we do; pray we must—mostly without uttering a single solitary syllable. Aiming a flashlight in the dark, a secret garden, a private chat room with God, surgery, scoring a touchdown in football, building a fire—when you look at it that way, apparently all we do in life is pray.

God will have it no other way.